# SPORT OF QUEENS

# SHE SAID/HE SAID

*These quotes from people in racing show while women are gaining recognition and equality in the industry, there is still a way to go to be treated as equals.*

'They bring me out at Spring Carnival time to pretend I'm getting a fair go.'

— RACECALLER VICTORIA SHAW

'I want to say to everyone else, get stuffed, because they think women aren't strong enough but we just beat the world.'

— JOCKEY MICHELLE PAYNE (after the 2015 Melbourne Cup)

'Michelle smashed another glass ceiling today.'

— PRIME MINISTER MALCOLM TURNBULL (after the 2015 Melbourne Cup)

'The real story was that it took fifteen years before another woman rode in the Melbourne Cup.'

— CHAMPION JOCKEY CLARE LINDOP (on her drought-breaking 2003 Cup ride)

'Without women, we'd struggle to have a jockey base.'

— NATIONAL JOCKEYS' TRUST NATIONAL MANAGER TONY CRISAFI

'Gender discrimination against female jockeys remains rife in Victorian racing. Trainers and their owners on major race days almost exclusively choose from a rigid hierarchy of male riders.'

— CONSTITUTIONAL LAWYER ERIC DYRENFURTH (*Sydney Morning Herald*)

'No-one can prove themselves unless they're given an opportunity and once the girls got the opportunity through the Apprentice Academy, they proved themselves every bit as good as the boys.'

— SOUTH AUSTRALIAN APPRENTICE ACADEMY TRAINING SUPERVISOR BILL FORRESTAL

'In this day and age when we've got close to twenty-five percent of women jockeys, it's absolutely vital the rights they have are as well-protected as any other person in the workforce.'

— AUSTRALIAN JOCKEYS' ASSOCIATION CHAIRMAN ROSS INGLIS

'The professional gambler is most hesitant to back a woman because she doesn't have the necessary vigor when it comes to using the persuader at the end of a race. Racing is really a man's sport.'

— FORMER BOOKMAKER BILL WATERHOUSE

'Women need to be acknowledged as an integral part of the growth of the racing industry.'

— LADIES IN RACING EDITOR CATHRYN MEREDITH

'I can be as good as a man but I can't be twice as good, which is often what I needed to be to get the ride. It was a hell of a fight to wear down the officials over twenty years.'

— GROUNDBREAKING QUEENSLAND JOCKEY PAM O'NEIL

'Women might be found wanting if they were to go on training year after year [but] might be good with quiet horses.'

— LEGENDARY MELBOURNE TRAINER JAMES SCOBIE

'I'm not a female jockey, I'm a fucking jockey.'

— NEW ZEALAND JOCKEY MAREE LYNDON

'It is most frustrating to educate and condition a horse on the track, then see the race ride go to a male jockey.'

— JOCKEY LESLEY BELLDEN (after becoming the first woman to ride a Randwick winner in 1983)

'Racing needs to stop being afraid of women with a voice.'

— JOURNALIST KRISTEN MANNING

'If we keep chipping away at the glass ceiling, it does crack.'

— CHAMPION SYDNEY TRAINER GAI WATERHOUSE

M

MELBOURNE BOOKS

Published by Melbourne Books
Level 9, 100 Collins Street,
Melbourne, VIC 3000
Australia
www.melbournebooks.com.au
info@melbournebooks.com.au



National Library of Australia
Cataloguing-in-Publication entry
Title: Sport of Queens: Women In Australian Horse Racing
Author: Shane McNally
ISBN: 9781925556193 (hardcover)
Subjects: Women in horse racing--Australia--History
Racehorse trainers--Australia--History
Women jockeys--Australia--History
Horse breeders--Australia--History

Cove photo: Royal Rumble, Clare Lindop, Morphettville, 2016 by Sharon Lee Chapman
sharonleechapmanphotography.fotomerchant.com
Printed in Singapore

## ACKNOWLEDGEMENT

Many thanks to all the women who took the time to tell their stories and the men prepared to comment.

Special thanks to Sharon Lee Chapman for providing many of the wonderful photos in this book, Mary Mountier for invaluable information on the women of New Zealand racing and Bradley Photographers for the image of the historic 2005 O'Hara sisters dead-heat. Thanks also to Kristen Manning, who has succeeded in a male-dominated domain, for the kind words.

Finally, Melbourne Books' David Tenenbaum deserves a special mention for recognising, as other publishers did not, that the stories of women in Australian racing deserved to be told.

# CONTENTS

# FOREWORD

What a privilege it is to be asked to provide the foreword for Shane McNally's *Sport of Queens* and how I enjoyed chatting with him as he undertook his extensive research, his passion for all things horse racing shining through.

Horse racing in Australia boasts proud traditions but sadly its history has more often than not been told through the eyes of men … about men. Women have been an oddity, an amusement, a side show to the main attraction.

Just take any Group One presentation for example. It's mostly men making the important speeches whilst female models strut and preen, their job purely and simply to look good, to provide eye-candy. Eye-candy for men that is, the target audience.

How out-dated is that!

Pick up a newspaper and look for a female tipster, good luck with that! Instead you can peruse the form guide for a female jockey — they are easier to find as they are labelled by their gender. As are, for reasons that have always alluded me, trainers and owners.

I have at times purposefully left the 'Miss', 'Ms' or 'Mrs' box unchecked when registering a share in a horse but mysteriously I always ended up labelled!

When searching for a new race name it is usually a male who is honoured: an administrator, trainer or jockey who has achieved great things. One would think watching from afar that no women have ever made significant contributions.

Which, of course, is nonsense — as Shane's work attests. He outlines the careers of many a great racing person who happens to be female.

I remember hearing, years ago, a jockey — it may have been Michelle Payne — saying that she knew real equality of treatment will have arrived when she is no longer referred to as a female rider.

Just a jockey. Like any other, asked to prove herself by talent and dedication alone.

I had the great privilege of writing, for Melbourne Books, the story of the 2015 Melbourne Cup winner Prince of Penzance whom Michelle Payne steered to a memorable victory.

While writing it I was wary of making too big a deal over Michelle's femaleness. Yes it was a great achievement, but how much do we go on about it before we become condescending?

Shane's work celebrates the achievements of racing women without belittling them. It is so wonderful to read about not only women who have been in the headlines but those we rarely hear about despite their great successes.

Often in the pages that follow Shane allows women to tell their stories in their own words and we share in their battles and glories. At the end of the day that is what we should all be focusing on, everything that is wonderful about horse racing, not the gender of those who make it great.

*Kristen Manning*

## PART I

# APPROACHING THE BARRIERS

## CHAPTER 1

# UNDER STARTER'S ORDERS

Scepticism was mixed with genuine excitement. The anticipation had reached fever pitch in the packed grandstands as the capacity field of tough old stayers milled around behind the barriers in the Morphettville home straight. It was standing room only on the Derby enclosure lawns. It was carnival time in Adelaide in the autumn of 1979 but this was different. The enthusiasm always reserved for feature racing was up a notch. A huge crowd had come out to see the running of the West End Stakes and virtually all eyes were on the visiting New Zealander carrying the red, white and blue stripes. Northfleet may not have attracted any extra serious money with the bookmakers but the presence of the young woman riding him brought another couple of thousand through the turnstiles, had the cameras clicking furiously and ensured the tote carried more than its share of mug wagers and spec bets.

She was a genuine racing curiosity, this Linda Jones. The 27-year-old mum had ridden more than fifty winners back home in New Zealand and recorded the first official

Australian win by a woman riding against men when she guided Pay The Purple to victory in the BTC Labour Day Cup at Doomben a week earlier. But hardcore racegoers were having none of this nonsense. The Adelaide Cup Carnival was in full swing and it would require strength, mettle and skill to beat hardened stayers and even harder jockeys.

The men of the silk and saddle would let the novelty rider set the tempo out in front on Northfleet and, when she did not manage to correctly judge the pace of the 2400 metre event, reel her in around the home turn. Only, she did, and they couldn't. Jones rated the tough Kiwi stayer perfectly in front, keeping her rivals off the bit in the middle stages and allowing the gelding more rein at the 600 metre mark before slipping them on the home turn. Northfleet turned for home more than two lengths clear and Jones pushed him out hands and heels to the post for an easy win. Australian racing would never be the same.

'They were pretty heady days and I know I was representing women in racing but all I really wanted to do was ride horses,' Jones said from her new home on the Sunshine Coast more than thirty years later.

'I'd just been half way around the country, treated as a celebrity at Rosehill on that first day riding in Australia and a winner in Brisbane, so by the time I got to Adelaide, the pressure was off. I got to enjoy the event. The crowd was buzzing and I had a few doubters, I suppose, but every woman in the stand was cheering for me even before we went into the starting gates.'

Amused at the assessments of her and other women riders as front-runners in those early days, Jones said she rode the way the horse dictated she needed to ride: 'Northfleet was a funny little horse who had to be ridden in front or he tended to give it away. So I led on him in Australia and quickly got a name as a front-running jockey. He settled well in the West End and I just tried to make him comfortable in the run and let him just roll along in front. When we came to the bend, he was travelling beautifully and I was still clear of the field and it was then that I realised we might win the race. I went for home on the bend but nothing really threatened us in the straight and the course just erupted as we went to the line.'

The crescendo of the race finish cheering turned to a mix of steady applause and disbelieving murmur as Jones brought Northfleet back to the mounting yard and the jockey was an instant headline around the country. They had photos of the winning rider attending to her two-year-old baby girl, pics of her and Alan hugging after the race, stories of how Linda Jones and Northfleet would be coming back for a tilt at the Melbourne Cup. Racetrack Magazine, the country's leading racing journal at the time, devoted its cover to a photo of Jones and champion rider Malcolm Johnston sharing a laugh at the races and women's magazines were clamouring to talk to the young blonde who could beat the men.

But change would not come easily and racing's inner sanctum were not prepared to accept the West End Stakes win as anything more than one of those upsets that occur all the time on racecourses. That historic 1979 feature race win, and Jones' earlier win in Brisbane's Labor Day Cup, may have nudged the door open for women on Australian racetracks but it hardly knocked down the walls.

With Linda and Alan Jones returning to New Zealand after Northfleet's saddle slipped in the Adelaide Cup and they finished unplaced, the media moved on to the next story. Without the headlines, women would face obstacles in the thoroughbred world for years to come — from the conservative racing clubs which still did not afford women full membership to the various licensing bodies which would put a hard pass mark on their applications and then the trainers and owners who simply wouldn't trust them with important rides.

The eighties was both frustrating and rewarding for women jockeys as they took two steps forward and one step back in their bid for equality. But weight of performance was forcing the establishment to accept them, if only slowly. The efforts of Pam O'Neill in Queensland and Beverley Buckingham in Tasmania paved the way for those to follow but they still had to work twice as hard as the men to earn their opportunities.

Women jockeys weren't getting a lot of rides in the early eighties but they were making the most of them. O'Neill rode a treble at the Gold Coast on her first day against the men and went on to a celebrated career; Buckingham won the Tasmanian jockey's premiership as early as 1982, rode five winners on the one Mowbray meeting in 1986 and is still regarded as one of the state's best-ever jockeys.

Despite Buckingham's ability to consistently command good rides in Tasmania, most women had to travel far and wide for the opportunity to just get on board a horse that was often simply making up the numbers. The winners came, though. Slowly and in out-of-the-way places, at non-TAB meetings and on bush tracks without anything that resembled a genuine grandstand, but they came.

Cheryl Neale was riding regular winners in Queensland while Debbie Lloyd garnered a strong following for her ability to win races on a regular basis on the South Australian provincial circuit. Women were increasingly putting their names in the record books. Carlene, Ramona and Leonie Wehr became the first sisters to fill all three placings in a race at Alice Springs in 1982. Monica Ryan rode four winners at Wondai in outback Queensland in 1990, with Jo Downes, Debbie Osborne and Jenny Cochrane chalking up the remaining three winners to make it a full card for women riders. In June of the same year, Maria Hunter rode eight straight winners over two meetings at Broome.

The winners continued to roll in even if the respect didn't automatically follow. In 1995, the Wondai achievement was replicated at a TAB meeting when Vanessa Hutchinson, Kim Arnold, Christine Puls and Maree Payne rode the card at Murtoa on the Victorian provincial circuit. Queensland country jockey Melissa Seagren went one better, achieving that feat all on her own on the bush track of Einasleigh in 2001 by booting home the program's six winners.

For all the hard work done by a new breed of race jockey, it could be argued the struggle these women endured and the sacrifices they made to overcome biases and achieve their rightful place in racing paled into insignificance alongside the woman now recognised as Australia's first female jockey. Wilhelmina Smith rode as Bill Smith at meetings across Far

North Queensland during the forties and fifties, a secret she kept until her death in 1975.

Wilhelmina's history remains clouded to this day, adding to the legend, with one story contradicting the other and confusion over the details and scope of her riding career. What is known is that she was born of English parents in Sydney and, following the death of her mother, grew up in a Perth orphanage after being abandoned by her father. She ran away from the orphanage and worked on the Adelaide wharves as a teenager before taking a ship to Cairns, where she dressed as a man and registered to ride in races.

She had a successful career on the bush circuit and kept her secret for more than twenty years in the saddle by never changing in front of the other jockeys and never showering until she went home. 'Bill' Smith was known as a loner and fellow riders just accepted 'his' eccentric ways and although rumour spread about the jockey's gender, it was put down as just that. Rumour. They regarded the softly-spoken Bill as an effeminate man, nicknamed him 'Girlie' and later 'Granny Smith' and never got close enough to strike up a friendship.

Along the way, the rewriting of history had Wilhelmina confused with early nineteen-hundreds' riding great W. H. Smith, winner of many of Australia's best races including a Victoria Oaks with which the pioneering woman is sometimes credited.

The reality, though, is a more compelling story than anything a win in that blue riband filly's classic could have ever produced. This was a time when women had limited rights and access on a racecourse and were certainly not considered strong or competent enough to match it with the men in the high pressure of a horse race. In the days before stewards' patrol film policed every inch of the action and professional punters and bookmakers analysed the footage of every runner in every race, only the toughest and shrewdest riders survived in the jockeying for position down the hundreds of hidden back straights across the country.

On the bush tracks, away from the gaze of the crowds, it was even tougher. No quarter was asked or given. The only concession Wilhelmina seemed to achieve was that changing room privacy, but it came at a price. It led to a lonely existence, rarely striking up a conversation with the other jockeys in the four or five hours of riding and waiting for the next ride at each race meeting. She kept her secret even as she lay on the track injured after a two-horse race fall at Atherton during the forties and refused the help of a fellow jockey who tried to remove her silks to help her breathe.

Wilhelmina Smith lived out her later years a recluse at Innot Springs on Queensland's Western Tablelands, died in poverty and was buried in an unmarked grave in the Herberton cemetery west of Cairns. Queensland racing writer Phil Purcer, who brought Wilhelmina's story to light through his racing website, was determined to pay tribute to the efforts of the woman who battled through her 'terribly sad life' just to do what women have the right to do today. Purcer approached the Herberton Lions Club for help with fundraising and, as more people began to learn and care about what Wilhelmina Smith had achieved against all odds, enough money was raised for a headstone to honour her life and achievements. It was unveiled in 2005.

While women were slowly accepted into the training ranks during the eighties, the stigma of backing a woman jockey remained. Brilliant Ballarat apprentice Therese Payne was outriding the boys on a regular basis in provincial Victoria and, when she got the opportunity, in Melbourne and Adelaide by the middle of that decade but was still considered a lucky 'sheila' by male punters. The fact that putting a line through Payne's name, or Buckingham's down in Tasmania, was actually costing punters money while they didn't think twice about supporting less competent male jockeys didn't seem to matter. Women couldn't ride, some punters figured, and no amount of wins or even a Tasmanian premiership was going to change their minds — women included.

Results would eventually soften racegoers' views about women riders but numbers would have a greater impact. A brilliant ride by Payne, Buckingham or visiting Kiwi champion Maree Lyndon, who rode with great success in Sydney during the late 1980s, could be rationalised as luck by someone with a bias they weren't about to surrender but what would they do when women jockeys dominated a race field? Not have a bet? That was unthinkable to rank and file punters so they eventually had to accept that women riders were here to stay and support them, financially if not philosophically.

After more than thirty-five years of riding against men, the percentage of women riders grows every year. The numbers are still down at metropolitan meetings but many provincial and country race fields have an even gender balance and, in many jurisdictions, teenage girls are entering into apprenticeships at a greater rate than boys.

In New South Wales, which was slow on the uptake to accept women riders, there are more female than male apprentices. The pattern continues around the country and South Australia's renowned Apprentice Academy is inundated with girls looking to make a career in race riding. With more than 100 female apprentices across the country, the future looks bright, suggesting the next generation of Australian racegoers will be watching and betting on races without considering the gender of the rider aboard.

The importance of the woman jockey cannot be underestimated in the drive for racing equality. For all the hard work that has gone unrecognised in racing offices, stables, breeding barns and even TAB agencies over many years, the emergence of the female jockey has been the driving force behind women's bid for equality in thoroughbred racing. She has also been the most visible symbol.

The tireless deeds of pioneers Wilhelmina, Linda, Pam, Bev and their sister jockeys have all played an integral role in the advancement of women in racing. So have the countless, nameless women who for decades rode silent trackwork on wet winter mornings across Australia without the hope of being rewarded with the mount on race day.

By the time sisters Tracy and Kathy O'Hara dead-heated for first in the Shoreline Restaurant Handicap at Gosford on 29 December 2005, women had the perfect photo to illustrate their story and celebrate their struggle. It was the definitive picture of the changing landscape of racing and there wasn't a man in sight.

# CHAPTER 2

# THE EARLY FORM

In November 1934, the *Australian Women's Weekly* ran with the headline 'Racing no longer the Sport of Kings'. The heading was a massive overstatement aimed at grabbing the attention of the magazine's female readership but the Melbourne Cup won by the great Peter Pan for the second time had three horses owned or part-owned by women, which the *Weekly* claimed was a major increase on previous years.

'Up to a year or two ago,' wrote its turf writer Jocelyn, the woman racehorse owner was 'rather a rarity ... but a change has come over the scene, even in one year.'

The first par of the article stated that while racing was 'formerly preserved for the nobility, women have gradually worked their way' and concluded with the suggestion the three pound, ten shillings a week upkeep made racing 'a privilege reserved for people of some means and leisure'. In other words: men.

By the forties, Canadian-born cosmetics queen Elizabeth Arden had become one of the leading owner-breeders in the US. She built up a strong stable of horses at her Maine Chance Farm and owned and bred 1947 Kentucky Derby winner Jet Pilot. She had run fourth the previous year with Lord Boswell, who went on to become a prominent sire. She had two more Derby runners and managed a fourth in 1954 with Jewel's Record but also owned champion forties filly Beaugay, outstanding colt Ace Admiral and Kentucky Oaks winner Fascinator. Arden is reported to have won $500,000 as an owner in 1945 alone and her deeds earned her the cover of *Time Magazine* in 1946 with the headline 'A queen rules the sport of kings.'

Women jockeys were starting to make inroads on minor circuits in the United States by 1950 but were still years away from riding at the major tracks and Australia was decades away from such a bold move. That year, Wanda Davis was described by visiting US journalist George McGann in Perth's *Sunday Times Magazine* feature as a 'pretty, young mother of two children' first and America's leading quarter horse rider second. He then said she had struck a major blow for women jockeys in 1949 when she beat champion hoop Johnny Longden in a match race at Mexico's Agua Caliente racecourse. As a sign of the times, the story named 'pretty' Margaret Griffin and 'pretty, young' Joyce Goldschmidt, who apparently cut an 'attractive figure', as other promising women riders.

Like the US, New Zealand was many years ahead of Australia in the equality stakes — so far ahead that when a woman from Hastings on the North Island became the first of her gender to train a Melbourne Cup winner in 1938, she couldn't put her name to the victory. Hedwick

'Granny' McDonald was forced to hand over the training of Catalogue to husband and accomplished jumps rider Allan, even though everyone knew she was putting the polish on the eight-year-old gelding. The Melbourne press acknowledged the horse was trained by a woman, the official trainer acknowledged it and so did the woman owner at every chance she got. It seems the only place where the feat was not recognised was in the official racebook.

'You know I am not the real trainer of Catalogue,' Allan McDonald told the press after the Cup win. 'My wife got the horse ready in New Zealand and it's only the last six weeks that he had been under my care. All credit for the win must go to my wife.'

Owner Mrs A Jamieson, who had been so angry at the Victoria Racing Club's stance that she threatened to scratch her horse from the great race in protest, confirmed it at the official ceremony: 'Granny McDonald should be standing here with me as the first woman to train a Melbourne Cup winner. She got him ready.'

There's a lot of conjecture over the impact the unrecognised Melbourne Cup had on Granny McDonald. While most people knew she was the real trainer — and even New Zealand Prime Minister Michael Savage sent her, and not husband Allan, a congratulatory telegram — her health deteriorated as she became increasingly dependent on alcohol in the years that followed. New Zealand's first-ever woman trainer, who set up a stable at Hastings in 1924 at the age of thirty-four and trained well over 300 winners, died of a stroke in 1959 at sixty-nine years old.

It's appropriate perhaps, that when a woman finally did

get credit for training the winner of our most famous race, the honour went to another New Zealander. In collecting the 2001 Melbourne Cup after the win of champion mare Ethereal, Sheila Laxon acknowledged in her acceptance speech as a tribute to McDonald that she was only the 'first official winner' of the great race and that the real honour belonged to her predecessor.

The women who paved the way for other women in Australian racing suffered too often for their efforts. Wilhelmina Smith and Hedwick McDonald are perhaps the most poignant cases but many of those who came after and achieved great success were also not given the same concessions men received for a bad ride or a run of poor form. If a man rode poorly, it was bad luck. If a woman turned in a bad ride, she proved women couldn't ride.

The achievements of women in racing dot the landscape from the early part of the twentieth century but the efforts were largely dismissed as a novelty or good luck. When champion three-year-old Patrobas backed up from his Victoria Derby win to take out the 1915 Melbourne Cup, Edith Widdis became the first woman to ever own the winner of our great race. Dorothy Sheil's efforts in the training ranks were more monumental, though, and led to a quick change in racing legislation. When she trained Precocious to win the 1932 VRC Grand National Steeplechase, relegating the legendary Mosstrooper to third place, her achievement was met with such concern that the racing body set about banning women from registering as trainers. It was just one feature win, and not a major flat race at that, but the establishment was taking no chances that this impetuous trend could continue.

It took more than another forty years before a woman would officially train a metropolitan winner in Australia. That honour went to Betty Lane, who had already proven herself for close to two decades training horses in the Western Districts of New South Wales. She had been rejected by the Australian Jockey Club many years earlier, with the reason given 'it's not our policy to license women'. This was despite the fact that Lane had mixed it successfully with the men on the country and provincial circuits for years. She was eventually granted a metropolitan permit in 1976 before becoming the first woman in Australia to have a Number One trainer's license in 1982.

Years earlier, though, Betty Shepherd is believed to have been the first licensed woman trainer. She trained out of Scone in New South Wales, keeping her stable to just two or three runners at a time, but she struck a huge blow for women when she took the best of them to Melbourne for the 1966 spring carnival. After showing a lot of staying promise, with the W. J. McKell Cup among his Sydney wins, Trevors came up against an outstanding Caulfield Cup field including turf greats Galilee and Tobin Bronze. He ran a slashing fourth before going on to finish midfield in the Melbourne Cup.

By the eighties, women were beginning to make their mark more regularly on the metropolitan circuit. Based in regional New South Wales, Deirdre Stein became the first woman to win a Group 1 race in Australia and she picked the best of them to win — Rising Prince bolted in with the 1985 Cox Plate to claim the WFA championship of Australia.

Four years later, a woman would claim Australia's greatest mile. Barbara Joseph saddled up talented three-year-old Merimbula Bay in the Doncaster Handicap but, despite winning the San Domenico Stakes the previous spring, was rated an outside chance at best. Joseph had been a licensed trainer, working out of Bombala in southern New South Wales, since 1975 and the Doncaster gave the trainer her biggest win. She moved her training operation to Canberra in 1994, where she now runs Joseph Jones Racing in partnership with Paul Jones, and has more than 1100 winners to her name.

The Cox Plate win didn't catapult Stein into the headlines for more than a few days, nor did the Doncaster create more than a Sunday press story about a woman training a roughie to win a feature. It did earn them added respect in some quarters but it had little bearing on the overall position of women trainers in the eighties.

CHAPTER 3

# MOVING UP

Things were changing slowly by the seventies and, while there was an element of male condescension about it, women were beginning to at least get the opportunity to participate in racing. In 1973, June Lossius became the first woman jockey to win a metropolitan race in Australia when she took out the Dame Merlyn Myer Transition aboard Some Attraction at Brisbane's Eagle Farm racecourse — albeit in a woman's only race. A year later, the VRC allowed women to be registered for 'ladies only' jockeys' races but the biggest change came across the Tasman a further four years on — when New Zealand's racing rules were amended to permit women jockeys to ride against men. This was the precursor to the Linda Jones phenomenon but thirty-something Queenslander Pam O'Neill was also pushing hard to force the officials to make changes.

Queensland became a leader in the advancement of women in the racing industry. O'Neill took years to finally gain her license to ride against men but wasted no time in proving her ability. She landed a winning treble on her first day of race riding at the Gold Coast in 1979, a world-first feat she achieved without the benefit of being able to claim a weight advantage now available to new riders serving an apprenticeship. At thirty-four, she was considered far too old to be an apprentice so she had to give away years of experience to the male riders without the benefit of the three-kilogram claim. But she kept winning anyway. A month later, she won her first feature race aboard Samei Boy in the Booroolong Handicap at Doomben. She went on to achieve great success in South-East Queensland and even beat legendary jockey Roy Higgins in a 'unisex' race in Melbourne.

'They used to run the occasional lady riders races but it was really nothing more than a gimmick just to attract crowds,' O'Neill recalls. 'I did ten barrier trials in one day before being allowed to ride, even though I'd ridden winners in restricted events all over Australia.'

The restrictions on women being involved in the most fundamental of racing duties was debilitating. Former husband Colin O'Neill went from leading rider to trainer in the seventies but Pam was very limited in the tasks she could perform for the stable.

'At one point there, I couldn't even touch a horse on a racetrack,' she recalls. 'I used to lead them up to the gate at Eagle Farm and hand them over to a man.'

'There was a lot of discrimination back then and after I started riding. When I started, I used to get changed in the doctor's rooms or a caravan. I would have got changed in a tent if necessary just to ride but it gives you an idea of what we were up against.

'I remember riding a horse a treat one day to win by a couple of lengths and an owner said if he put a bloke on it he'd have won by four. There was this attitude that women weren't strong enough but I could hold horses in a race that males couldn't hold.

'At one point, it didn't matter how much you proved yourself, they wanted more. I always said I can be as good as a man but I can't be twice as good, which is often what I needed to be to get the ride.'

Linda Jones may have captured most of the headlines at the time but O'Neill had done much of the groundwork to give women the chance to ride in races. She doesn't resent the attention her good friend received but remembers feeling a little cheated that the rules prevented her from riding earlier: 'Linda and I are good mates and I remember giving her my saddle to ride in one race and having to stand in the enclosure to watch her,' she recalls.

O'Neill wasn't the only jockey pushing to for the chance to ride against men. Toowoomba's Iris Nielsen was one of a group of women who travelled throughout Queensland, New South Wales and Victoria to compete in 'ladies' races to further the cause. Once women were licensed to ride against men, she proved her case beyond doubt and became the leading rider in the South-East Queensland/Northern Rivers area. She won more than 100 races before being killed in a race fall at Lismore in March 1988. The Iris Nielsen Ladies Invitational Cup is run annually at Ballina in her memory.

The eighties was an era of great advancement in Queensland for women in racing. Dianne Moseley furthered the push when she became the first woman to win a Group 1 race in Australia, taking out the rich Doomben Cup aboard New Zealander, Double You Em in 1982. It was a victory of sorts for women riders before the barriers even opened — Moseley had secured the ride on a genuine chance in the race instead of being forced to pick up a mount nobody else wanted.

The prominence of the Queensland woman jockey enabled them to outride the men at many provincial and country meetings from the 1980s onwards. After the Wondai whitewash of 1990, it took another twenty years for the feat to be repeated — this time it was at a TAB meeting. It was January 2010, when Alisha Taylor rode a treble aboard Country Sherrif, Fire Hazard and Malicious Gal at Rockhampton. Carly-Mae Pye rode a double and Trinity Bannon and Shayla Evans picked up the other two races to make it a clean sweep for women.

While Moseley was riding in the best races, trainer Carmel Richardson won the Toowoomba Cup three times in five years from 1981 with Odd Spot. When she won the Cup with Lord Woden in 1985, Tod Minor gave her the feature double by winning the Weetwood Handicap.

Moseley's deeds paved the way for a string of quality women riders. Bernadette Cooper arrived on the scene in 1990 and won the Dux of the Apprentices School in 1993 before going on to win more than 300 races. She is now a respected media personality and form analyst.

After Cooper came Lacey Morrison. She finished high up on the Brisbane jockeys' premiership in the early 2000s and Mandy Radecker became the first female to win the Brisbane apprentices' premiership in 2007–08.

Western Australia didn't provide a great deal of scope for women but those who ventured into the male-dominated field made the most of their opportunities. Alana Samson arrived in the late nineties — years behind some other states — and opened the door for those to follow with immediate success and more than 400 winners. Brilliant apprentice Lucy Warwick burst onto the Perth scene in 2014 and rode 267 winners in just over two years before shocking the racing world with her decision to take an indefinite break from race riding. The news came soon after finishing second to riding great William Pike in the 2015–16 premiership. In a statement released in September 2016, Warwick's manager Dale Verhagen said the industry demands had taken their toll on the young rider's health.

'Lucy, after consultation with her family, has decided to take an indefinite break from racing,' the statement read. 'In recent times the demands of the industry, in particular continuous wasting ... [have] inhibited her ability to ride at the standard that she has set herself.'

While the general consensus was the break would not be a long-term move, it highlighted the pressures facing a teenager in just her second year of riding. Her absence left a massive void in the ranks of women riders out West, with the 2016–17 premiership boasting an all-male top-ten riders list.

While other states made their move, Australia's two premier states were unwilling to change with the times. In Victoria, the likes of Rhonda Comitti battled away with consistent winners on the provincial circuit but wasn't given a chance in the city.

Even as recently as the early 2000s, New South Wales was a reluctant participant. Robyn Freeman spent four years with the Waterhouse stable in Sydney as a young rider but trips abroad to Macau in 2006 and then South Africa did not bring the rewards many men have achieved. When she returned from overseas, she struggled to get any foothold in either Sydney or Melbourne and has since based herself at Albury to make a living.

The two largest states have hardly been progressive in their attitude towards women, particularly jockeys, but they are slowly making headway. Michelle Payne, after all, did get the Melbourne Cup ride to provide the opportunity and, in New South Wales, Kathy O'Hara regularly commands good books at metropolitan meetings. And, in 2014, every jockey at a non-TAB meeting at Orange was a woman. Of course, that mark needs to be put in perspective: it was a country track and the TAB didn't cover it.

Tasmania has for years been a different story. It was quick to acknowledge the rare ability of a teenager who would take all before her. English-born Beverley Buckingham won her first race at just her fourth ride at Elwick Racecourse in Hobart in 1980 and went on to win twenty-two races for the season. It was just the beginning. The following season, she won sixty-three races and became the first female anywhere in the world to win a state's jockeys premiership. She was just seventeen.

Buckingham rode 906 winners during an eighteen-year career, and collected most of Tasmania's best races along the way, including three Hobart Cups. She won the Tasmanian premiership three times and set a state record of 109 winners in the 1995–96 season. She became the first woman in the Southern Hemisphere to win 1000 races. The sparkling career — the benchmark for all woman jockeys to come — ended suddenly and shockingly when Buckingham broke her neck in a race fall at Elwick in May 1998. She was unable to use her arms and legs and was told she would be quadriplegic for life. She spent three months in rehabilitation in Victoria before returning home to the family property of Brigadoon in Tasmania, where an intensive rehabilitation program continued. She has defied the odds and managed to overcome the worst of the crippling injury to walk again, with difficulties, and trained her first winner at Albury in October 2003. Buckingham was inducted into the Tasmania Racing Hall of Fame in 2005.

Today's women jockeys, Buckingham included, owe a lot to Queenslander O'Neill who, with the help of the visiting Linda Jones, brought enough pressure to change the rules. Their efforts forced officials to grant women the right to ride against men in 1979. Until then, women had to ride in 'ladies' races and in amateur events.

The firsts continued after O'Neill and Buckingham. Clare Lindop became the first to win a metropolitan mainland premiership in 2005 and, the same year, Andrea Leek literally overcame more obstacles when she became the first woman to win a Grand National Hurdle at Flemington.

Without the deeds and the determination O'Neill showed back in the seventies and early eighties against great odds, these great achievements may not have been accomplished.

'I had to go in fully fledged against the men,' O'Neill

recalls. 'Whereas other riders starting out would be able to claim, I wasn't afforded that luxury. I said I can be as good as a man but I can't be twice as good, which is often what I needed to be to get the ride. But I think I made the most of the rides I did get.'

Indeed she did. O'Neill rode 400 winners, including several in the United States in 1980, before retiring at fifty-two. She is still actively involved in racing as a director of the Queensland branch of the Australian Jockeys Association.

## CHAPTER 4

# TAKING AN EARLY LEAD

It's fitting that New Zealand, despite a slow start, would become one of the world leaders in the acceptance of women in thoroughbred racing. It was the first country in the world in which women voted in a federal election. That was 1893 and it followed a long, hard-fought campaign by one of the world's great suffrage movements led by Kate Sheppard and the foresight of political leaders like nineteenth century Premier Sir Robert Stout and his social reformer wife Anna Paterson Stout.

If anything, it's a little surprising that it took such a progressive country another eighty-four years to acknowledge women had the right to ride against men in races. Of course, Hedwick McDonald led the way for female trainers as early as the 1930s but, while some notable women began to train, they hardly rushed to take up the role in the forty years after that.

Women jockeys were still referred to as 'lady riders' in October 1970, when the so-called Powder Puff Derby was run at Tauranga. The name of the race may have been condescending at the time and down-right comical these days but women would take any opportunity they could get to ride in competition. The race attracted eleven women, including future groundbreaking rider Linda Jones, who won aboard Scots Bard and went on to campaign vigorously for equal rights for women in horse racing.

While Jones attracted so much hype in New Zealand and on her first trip to Australia, Canadian Joan Phipps was the first woman to ride against men in an actual open-betting race there. It was Melbourne Cup Day 1977 but it was being run 2600 kilometres east of Flemington, just south of Auckland in the Waikato district. Phipps was up against nineteen male riders in the Te Hinemoa Handicap at Te Awamutu, riding an outsider called Daphalee. It was a tough assignment, reportedly made tougher by the attitude of many of her rivals, but she remained focused throughout the day and came out an unlikely winner.

'They didn't want me there,' Phipps said years later. 'None of the jockeys talked to me. I just stayed focused.'

Daphalee and Phipps won in a three-way photo finish. Her resolve, rather than the fear of the men against whom she was competing, prevailed. Ultimately it helped change the course of thoroughbred racing in this part of the world forever.

Building on Phipps' great work, several women began to ride against the men within the year. Four women made their professional riding debuts at two courses on 15 July 1978. Joanne Hale, Joanne Lamond and Sue Day all picked up rides at Waimate, while Vivienne Kay rode at Trentham. One week later, Day became the first New Zealand woman to win against the men at Waimate.

Within months, Linda Jones became a sensation, not just in Australia but at home. She had come a long way since winning the Powder Puff Derby and even in the two years since the New Zealand Racing Conference conveniently dismissed her as being 'too old and too weak' when she first applied for a license in 1976. She was twenty-four.

It all changed in 1977 when the New Zealand Parliament again showed a leaning towards the progressive and passed the Human Rights Bill outlawing sexual discrimination. Jones finally had the right to ride against men but pregnancy delayed her start by a year. She won her first race aboard husband Alan's horse Big Bickies at Te Rapa in August 1978 and went on to tie for second in the New Zealand Jockeys' Premiership. She was the first woman in Australia or New Zealand to win a classic when she took out the now defunct Wellington Derby at Trentham aboard Holy Toledo. Despite that overwhelming success, Jones and other women riders were forced to change in caravans, switchboard rooms and any space available. One of the reasons given to Jones for rejection when she first applied for a license, in fact, was that clubs would have no changing rooms for women. The officials, who somehow hadn't considered building new change rooms, were actually serious.

Jones had a short but spectacular career. She was on the front page of newspapers in New Zealand and, during her 1979 visit to Australia, the image of her sharing a laugh with champion rider Malcolm Johnston became one of the iconic covers of *Racetrack Magazine*. She won sixty-five races before breaking her neck in a track gallop in March 1980. While she recovered from her injuries, she gave away race riding to help run the family stable at Cambridge and raise daughter Clare, but others would continue the legacy.

Maree Lyndon emerged as an outstanding rider and proved it both sides of the Tasman. She was a leading Sydney rider for Kiwi trainer Brian Smith and the first woman to win a 3200 metres feature in Australia when she piloted grand stayer Lord Reims to victory in the 1987 Adelaide Cup. The win wouldn't be enough to change the mindset of the broader racing establishment for very long. Lyndon was something of a victim of the added scrutiny many Australian women had experienced on smaller stages when she became the first woman to ride in a Melbourne Cup later that year. Her mount Argonaut Style became unsettled the moment he entered the mounting yard: he sweated up badly and became so fractious that he even bucked on the way to the starting gates. The horse missed the jump and finished second last to Kensei. While international superstar Frankie Dettori and Cup winner Michael Kinane, among others, could be excused for bewildering rides in different Cups, the same latitude was not afforded Lyndon. She was on a horse that had run its race before the start and was blamed for that. She wouldn't get another ride in the race.

In a career that spanned more than a decade, Lyndon won the Group 1 New Zealand Cup as well as two races at the highest level in Australia before winning a further eighty races on the highly competitive Asian circuit. This was at a time when most women weren't being given any decent rides and Lyndon fought hard to get enough chances to carve out a glittering career. While she was very successful riding in Malaysia, her health deteriorated with a mystery illness and she lost eight kilograms before returning home. Her condition improved but her enthusiasm for race riding was waning. After recording her biggest career win aboard Miss Stanima in the Auckland Cup in January 1990, she married that September and retired the following month.

Linda Ballantyne would achieve a better result when she became the second woman to ride in a Melbourne Cup two years later. She rode New Zealander Plume D'Or Veille into a respectable eighth place. She won seven races on the tough stayer and also rode him in the Brisbane and Sydney Cups. Ballantyne rode with great success in Singapore and Malaysia in the late nineties but her best successes came at home. She recorded Group 1 wins in the Kelt Capital Sakes on The Message and the Manawatu Sires' Produce aboard outstanding juvenile Cordero and became the first woman in Australia or New Zealand to win a million-dollar race when she piloted Rua Rukana to victory in the 1991 Trentham Magic Millions Classic.

The list of outstanding New Zealand women riders began to grow, with Debbie Healey riding around 500 winners in the early eighties. Kim Clapperton then rode with great success on the Malaysian circuit in the early- to mid-nineties. She went from becoming the first female to win the New Zealand Apprentice Jockeys' Premiership to take out the 1993 Singapore Jockeys' Premiership, then capped an outstanding career there with a win in the 1995 Singapore Gold Cup aboard Grand Jury. Clapperton was only nineteen when she arrived on the Malaysian peninsula. She went on to win fifteen classic or feature races over six seasons but the Gold Cup was the biggest of them and she still remembers the roar of the crowd as they turned into the Kranji straight.

'I was right up there throughout and I went into the straight knowing I was a real chance,' she recalls. 'The first three horses across the line were for my trainer Teh Choon Beng and the added pressure was that I had the choice of rides. It was a massive, massive crowd and a very vocal crowd and they let you know if you didn't ride well. It was a tough run up the straight, I remember, and it was a three-way finish with only a head or so between them.'

Clapperton went on to become the first woman to ever ride in Hong Kong, then worked and rode in England, France and the United States.

'It was a great experience but I was riding against the established jockeys and didn't always get good horses,' she says. 'In Hong Kong, they made a huge fuss of me because I was the first woman to ride there and had me parading at length before my first ride in a feature race. All that managed to do was stir up my horse no end and we did well to finish sixth. It was a great experience riding work at Newmarket on the Heath and Longchamp was amazing, although it's a big course to ride when you're on a slow horse. But for that era, as a woman riding on some of the best tracks in the world, I took any ride I could get.'

While Clapperton conquered the Malaysia circuit, South Islander Catherine Tremayne quickly established herself as one of New Zealand's outstanding jockeys in the nineties. She rode six winners on one day at Ruakaka and her feature race wins included the Ellerslie Sires' Produce and the New Zealand Oaks.

Lisa Cropp won the 2005–06 and 2006–07 New Zealand

Jockeys' Premierships but her exceptional achievements of having ridden 970 winners including seven at Group 1 level have been subsequently tainted by controversy. She tested positive to using methamphetamine and has battled drug-related issues in recent years. In a sad irony, Cropp's potential career-ending ban came after she failed to produce a drug test under controversial circumstances at Te Awamutu in 2014 — the course on which Joan Phipps created history almost forty years earlier. Cropp is currently serving a three-year ban.

The fact that the deeds of successful women in New Zealand racing no longer creates headlines is a healthy sign, according to Mary Mountier, author of *Racing Women of New Zealand*. She says the huge success of woman jockeys, in particular, makes New Zealand a world leader in racing equality.

'The fact that female riders who win major races in New Zealand are seldom commented on is paradoxically good news,' she explains. 'It reflects their position as equals in a male-dominated industry. While New Zealand was one of the last western countries to allow women to become professional jockeys, we are now seen as a world leader in providing riding opportunities on the basis of skill, not sex.

'Females are regularly among the top ten on jockeys' premierships, and have headed the list four times since 2005. When pioneers like Linda Jones proved their worth on the racetrack, early scepticism faded away. Today, racing could hardly function here without them, with females making up at least forty percent of apprentices each year.

'New Zealand has always allowed women to train their

own horses, but the first professional trainer gained her license in 1924. This was Granny McDonald. Back home, she got due credit for Catalogue's 1938 Melbourne Cup win, and subsequently there have been many successful female trainers, some in their own right and others in partnership with a male. Again, their success is so commonplace that it is not considered newsworthy.'

It wasn't always that way. In the mid-twentieth century, women had better success entering training rather than riding ranks but they still had plenty of opposition and often had to train their own horses.

Joyce Edgar Jones followed soon after Macdonald, but was a small owner–trainer until she bought her own property at South Canterbury in the forties. She bred 1950 Caulfield Cup winner Grey Boots and reached the high-point of her career when she trained Sailing Home to win the 1972 Auckland Cup. Edgar Jones bred and owned the outstanding mare, who won several other major races that season, and she was named New Zealand Racing Personality of the Year — the first time a woman had received the honour.

Another great pioneer, Laurel Campbell became a licensed trainer in 1927. She overcame tragedy to become a prolific trainer of jumpers over thirty years when her six-year-old daughter and only child was hit by a truck and killed in 1935. Campbell's greatest win came when Bandmaster won the 1951 Grand National at Riccarton. In her later years, she suffered from depression and died in a Christchurch psychiatric hospital in 1971.

Freda White was another great conditioner of jumpers and wrote herself into New Zealand folklore through the deeds of two of her horses. The first came in the 1951 Mariri Steeplechase at Trentham. Kentucky Flight had set up a huge lead but stumbled at the last fence and dislodged Fred Cleaver — only for the jockey to remount, chase down the new leader and record a remarkable win. In 1974, Teak won the Hawkes Bay Steeplechase at his seventh attempt at the race. He was a rising sixteen year old.

Margaret Bull was the first great woman trainer of the New Zealand modern era. After preparing the outstanding Longfella on an owner/trainer's permit to win the Ellerslie and Manawatu Sires Produce Stakes and four other races during the 1971–72 season, she became a licensed trainer in 1972 and went on to train more than 500 winners.

Bull is best remembered in Australia for an historic 1985 two-state Group 1 double. She took class galloper Lacka Reason to Flemington to win the Turnbull Stakes, then found a closed-circuit TV and watched her outstanding miler Magnitude run in the Epsom Handicap at Randwick half an hour later. The five-year-old Amalgam gelding was ridden by glamour jockey Malcolm Johnston and, with good form back in New Zealand, was sent out a 14/1 chance in the capacity field of twenty. Johnston rode a forward race and sent the visitor to the lead as they topped the Randwick ride at the 300 metre mark and, for a moment, Bull was worried he'd gone too early. The move was the right one, though, with Magnitude holding on for a half-length win over the fast-finishing Colour Page and favourite Double Dandy.

Since then, New Zealand has produced many top-level women trainers. Welsh-born Sheila Laxon, who arrived in New Zealand in 1980, achieved her greatest success when she took Ethereal to Melbourne in 2001 and transformed the mare from a class Queensland Oaks-winning filly to a champion mare with wins in the Caulfield and Melbourne Cups. Before that, she was the regular trackwork rider of Empire Rose for her former husband Laurie Laxon before the giant mare won the 1988 Melbourne Cup. Three years later, she overcame a near-fatal fall in 1991 that left her in a coma for a week and forced her to learn how to walk, talk and ride again over the following year.

Laxon was a sensation in Australia in the Spring of 2001. She got the daughter of Rhythm-Romanee Conti ready with a couple of placed runs at Pukekohe and Matamata, then arrived in Melbourne unheralded before the mare ran a slashing third in the Caulfield Stakes. It was enough to make Ethereal equal favourite for the Caulfield Cup a week later and she narrowly beat Sky Heights. She went on to wear down tear-away Godolphin stayer Give the Slip and high-class Irish visitor Persian Punch in the Melbourne Cup at her next start and, the following Autumn, Laxon brought the champion back to win the Group 1 BMW at Rosehill.

More recently, Lisa Latta set a new mark when she became the first woman training on her own to win the New Zealand Trainers Premiership in 2013–14. The Central Districts trainer has around 100 horses in work and has trained the winners of well over 800 races and sixteen million dollars.

Mountier says that while female jockeys and even trainers had to battle hard for their rights, women have been traditionally better accepted on committees and in administrative roles: 'I think women in those areas always had less opposition than the competitive roles of riding and training. In recent times, female input is actively encouraged around board tables.'

Today, New Zealand has its strongest ever contingent of women riders. Lisa Allpress was the nation's top jockey of either gender for the 2015–16 season with a massive 171 winners. That figure needs to be analysed to be fully appreciated. She achieved it despite being out twice through lengthy suspensions and an injury after a fall at Otaki in November 2015 or she may have given James McDonald's New Zealand record of 207 winners in a season a shake. Allpress has won two premierships, ridden more than 1200 winners and topped the 100 mark in five separate seasons.

Danielle Johnson may yet break that record. She has been in the top five jockeys in the country for the past four seasons and, barely in her mid-twenties, looks certain to claim one if not multiple premierships sooner rather than later. Kelly McCullough, Alysha Collett, Samantha Wynne, Samatha Collett and Rosie Myers finished the 2016–17 season either inside or just outside the top ten on the national premiership.

Women make up virtually half of the top ten jockeys list, even though Allpress has been missing through injury. The champion was in Tokyo on a three-month stint leading up to the 2016 Japan Cup when she sustained multiple injuries including a fractured tibia after falling from a juvenile. Further down the list are former leading rider Sam Spratt and Trudy Thornton, a fifty-something veteran of more than thirty years and over 1000 winners.

The one thing that stands out in a review of the New Zealand Jockeys Premiership is not just the number of winners but the number of rides women are securing. It gives a clear indication that New Zealand's best women are achieving far greater recognition than those struggling just to get city rides in Australia's eastern states.

For all the credit New Zealand deserves, though, its Hall of Fame still tells a story of women not being fully recognised. The honour roll features many champion horses, dozens of well-deserving men and Linda Jones. There's no Hedwick Macdonald, no Sheila Laxon, no Margaret Bull. Perhaps they are now ready for consideration, along with some world-class jockeys who just happen to be women.

## CHAPTER 5

# MAINTAINING THE PACE

Half of the top ten Adelaide jockeys at any one time are usually women. What that tells us is that, while they may be struggling for recognition in Melbourne, Sydney and elsewhere, women get a fair go in South Australia.

Clare Lindop has won three premierships, Jamie Kah has won it once and is expected to add several more to the list. It's not as though South Australia has a poor group of male riders — far from it. Dominic Tourneur, Jason Holder, Matthew Neilson, Joe Bowditch and Paul Gatt could hold their own anywhere. It's just that they have to compete for their rides on a far more level playing field than their eastern states colleagues.

In Adelaide, owners and trainers know that Lindop, Kah, Emily Finnegan, Caitlin Jones and young Eran Boyd are available. The first two have proven themselves to be elite riders and the others are establishing themselves of jockeys of quality.

It's something of a self-fulfilling prophecy. The women

riders have been given more opportunities, from the South Australian Apprentice Academy onwards, and have made the most of them. Connections see the results and note the quality of the rides and there's no reason to discount a jockey based on gender.

South Australia has been a goldmine for women riders in recent years and produced some of the best riders anywhere in the world — including Lindop and Kah. An obscure meeting at Mount Gambier in early 2015 provided the exclamation mark to a state's great support of female participation when women rode the eight-race card. Apprentice Emily Finnegan rode a treble, Clare Lindop and Holly McKechnie won doubles and another apprentice Chelsea Jokic picked up the other race.

The benefits and respect the current crop enjoys owes a lot to the efforts of a strong and talented group of women jockeys who did it tough during the eighties and nineties. Debbie Lloyd and Penny Fox were South Australian pioneers back in the early eighties and Ruth McMillan, Reagan Rayner, Annmarie White, Marie Bouldon and Angela Barr carried on the good work and paved the way for the next generation.

There were others too, who paid a high price for their part in the advancement of the riding scene for South Australian women. Michelle Lavars is confined to a wheelchair after a fall just before the winning post at Penola back in 1992 left her a paraplegic. After recovering from a horror fall at Oakbank in 2002, Cheree Buchiw lost the bottom portion of her leg in a freak accident when her mount went through the aluminium running rail at Cheltenham the following year. Anne-Marie Wilkinson became a quadriplegic after a fall in a hurdle race at Murray Bridge in 1996.

When Ruth Ashley was riding under her maiden name of MacMillan, she was too busy searching for rides and then turning them into winners to consider herself an emissary for those to come. When she started riding as a sixteen year old in 1984, she didn't mind the very long and very early hours just to have a job doing what she loved, even if it meant less rides than her male counterparts who she believes may not have even worked as hard.

'I really do believe the girls back then had a harder and tougher work ethic than the boys,' she recalls. 'I'm not sure whether it was to get the chance to ride in races but I remember working very hard and not minding it. We worked harder back then than the apprentices need to do today but that was more than thirty years ago and I'm pretty sure that's the same for everyone in racing.

'I worked from 3am and did trackwork every morning because that's what I needed to do to get rides. I didn't have much trouble picking up rides while I still had my three-kilo claim but it got tougher later on.'

While she established herself as a respected jockey with great strength, Ashley remembers having to virtually prove herself again when returning after childbirth. Despite winning something like 250 races and finishing a narrow second in an apprentice's premiership after missing a month, the thirty-something Ruth MacMillan ran into obstacles when she tried to renew her license. She was told she would have to return as a B-class rider, although special dispensation would be granted if she picked up city rides.

'I remember having a decent fight with the stewards after that,' she says. 'I told them I was an A-class jockey before I had the baby and I was an A-grade rider. I virtually had to threaten them with the laws relating to coming back to work after maternity leave before they gave me my A-class license. That's one area where you just know a male rider wouldn't experience the same issues.

'I have no doubt things have definitely improved in that area. I think the girls are well treated today but they've worked for it. You won't get many people with a better work ethic than Clare Lindop, who worked her arse off to prove herself before she got the chance to prove herself and eventually become the great rider she is today.'

Another of the women to have worked to set the new standard is Jamie Kah, the premiership winning jockey who looks to have multiple titles at her mercy in the years ahead. She won the title in 2012–13 premiership as an eighteen-year-old in only her second season then, after having a break to deal with the pressures associated with such immediate success, has returned and taken her riding to even greater levels. The two-time winner of the John Letts Medal for South Australia's best jockey is confident the playing field for South Australian jockeys is as even as it is anywhere in the world.

'I think it's pretty even now,' Kah says. 'In South Australia, I'd say it's equal opportunity. You might still find some owners who would rather have a male jockey but they're a dying breed. Most smart owners and trainers would pick the best jockey, regardless of their gender. In Melbourne, they may be a bit boy-centric from what I hear but then they have so many great male riders. I think I'd struggle to go there and convince connections to take off Craig Williams or Damien Oliver but I'd hope the same would apply if they came over here.'

If the state is as fair as Kah believes it is, a man who for more than fifteen years ran the South Australian Apprentice Academy can take a lot of the credit for it. Recently retired steward and training supervisor Bill Forrestal encouraged and promoted girls to become riders when most other states were looking for boys only. Under Forrestal's watch, teenage girls flocked to the Academy to get the opportunity they weren't getting elsewhere.

'When I started running the Apprentice Academy about fifteen years ago, there were considerably more boys than girls but, around 2008 when there were sixteen apprentices, it was the first time there were equal numbers,' Forrestal says. 'Of that group, several of the girls were very talented who were prepared to work hard and that laid the foundation for female apprentices to make inroads. They won over the trainers with their work ethic and right through to this day, South Australian trainers and owners have been happy to put girls on their horses. About ten years ago, we brought in the extra training sessions on a Friday afternoon and that was a period of time where the girls seized the opportunity. They worked very hard riding trackwork at every opportunity and I'd have to say they worked as hard if not harder than the boys.'

The female apprentices weren't just making up the numbers for the sake of equality, they were leading the way. Libby Hopwood and Amy Herrmann won the Dux of the

Apprentice Academy twice each and Jamie Kah and Kristal Bishop both took the honour once.

'We had built this wonderful initiative with Singapore and the great thing about winning our Dux was that it gave each of those girls a trip to Singapore to ride for two weeks,' Forrestal recalls. 'It gave them the chance to experience riding elsewhere, against some of the best jockeys in the world, and several of our girls won races over there.

'Libby and Amy led the way for the next era of female apprentices and they've outnumbered the boys over the past eight years. At one stage, I had seventeen girls and five boys in the Academy. I remember being interviewed by a Melbourne journalist at the time and saying I wondered where the next boy was going to come from.

'Some of those girls have become outstanding jockeys, probably none more than Jamie Kah, who in my opinion was the best apprentice in Australia when she won the premiership against the senior riders in 2013.'

Forrestal believes that while it has many quality senior jockeys, Adelaide is recognised as a place in which it is far easier to compete for rides away from the boiler room of Melbourne and Sydney, where trainers had access to some of the world's most proven jockeys.

'I've been contacted many times by aspiring young riders, male and female, who couldn't get a go interstate and were looking for an opportunity,' he says. 'It wasn't just Victoria that showed interest either. We had them coming from Tasmania and Queensland. Siggy Carr was one of our great success stories, gaining a lot of experience here before returning home to Tasmania. Adelaide was becoming recognised as a place where trainers were prepared to give apprentices a go and it wasn't just that, I had a great relationship with the media and they were enthusiastic about doing stories on the female apprentices in particular.

'I worked with apprentices for fifteen years and I was in the industry for forty years and I never honestly say I never once had a need or an inclination to treat the female and male apprentices any differently. Hopefully that's now the standard rather than the exception. But the word around Australia for some years now, I believe, is that the girls get an opportunity in South Australia.'

## CHAPTER 6

# JOCKEYING FOR POSITION

Even as women have come into the world racing spotlight, it seems the spotlight is often out of focus. They are often judged as being a first for women or for matters unrelated to their trade. Jockeys are judged by their ability to present or speak well or for how attractive they may be. Australian women riders — arguably the best in the world — somehow often don't even feature in the international debate.

In 2016, the international website 'ranker.com' listed the top women jockeys of the world and somehow managed to put only one Australian-based jockey — predictably Michelle Payne after winning the Melbourne Cup — in the seventeen who were rated. She came in at thirteen, eight places behind expat Kayla Star, who has ridden with some success in the United States. Triple Adelaide premiership winning jockey Clare Lindop didn't rate a mention and nor did Kathy O'Hara, Linda Meech, Katelyn Mallyon or Jamie Kah.

England's Clare Balding topped the list for her deeds

as a journalist and Canadian Chantal Sutherland was ranked number two for being a 'model, television personality' and for her 'appearances on reality TV shows'. In fairness, Sutherland is an accomplished rider but her record hardly puts her in the same league as Lindop and Payne. Balding was a good amateur jockey from a top racing family and is a very good writer but her deeds in the saddle don't warrant inclusion on the list, let alone top billing.

Any question about the credentials of the Australian women is quickly answered by the simple fact they ride every day in a country that has more race meetings than anywhere on the planet against men who have proven to be at least the equal and usually superior to their overseas counterparts. They don't ride in 'ladies only' races, they are still forced to overcome a diminishing bias and they are figuring highly on jockeys premierships.

It's a major triumph for women, considering they have only been allowed to ride against men since the late seventies, then went right through the eighties struggling to get a metropolitan ride against proven male jockeys — who even the most open-minded owner would have chosen for their sheer experience and record — and had to work harder than most men to secure rides by the nineties.

From O'Neill to Lyndon, Therese Payne and Buckingham through to Lindop and O'Hara, the struggle continued with varied levels of success. Even when there was great success, it was often short-lived. Rachel Mason became the first woman to ride four winners in a day in Brisbane in 2005 but could only take her career metro tally to thirty-seven as the rides stopped coming.

It wasn't just a case of women having to prove their right to ride in quality races, they genuinely faced that issue — male riders who had 1000 winners and a string of Group 1s under their belt would obviously be chosen ahead of an inexperienced woman. Who would chose any rider of potential, male or female, when they had the opportunity to book Shane Dye, Darren Beadman, Damien Oliver or Craig Williams? That question was the focus of the 2011 Caulfield Cup, when the accomplished Lindop was removed from Southern Speed for the great 2400 metres handicap and replaced with Williams. Lindop had earned the right to ride the star mare but the owners had the right, even against trainer Leon Macdonald's advice, to replace her. Southern Speed won courtesy of a faultless ride by Williams, clearly one of the world's best jockeys, and the argument was silenced. Lindop may have achieved the same result but it's doubtful any rider anywhere could have piloted the mare better. Similarly, it's as close to a certainty as can be argued that Prince of Penzance would not have won the 2015 Melbourne Cup without the Michelle Payne ride.

Whether it's a bias of ignorance or a cold calculation, the only way Australian women riders have been able to overcome the mindset is to wear away slowly with results — and the only way to achieve the results is by making the most of gradually increasing opportunities.

Even today, as women win premierships and Group 1 races from often restricted opportunities, the mindset continues. There are still many trainers all around Australia who genuinely believe women can't handle the pressure of a big race and won't put them on a top horse.

Despite those setbacks, the list of quality women riders continues to grow as even the most conservative racegoers gradually forget to question the gender of the rider. Since Linda Jones and Pam O'Neill set the mark in the late seventies, the barriers have slowly come down on a state-by-state basis. Sydney racing has come a long way since Jane Spence broke through for women at Canterbury in 1983. Kathy O'Hara has been a major player for years, while Jess Taylor and apprentice Deanne Panya are regular city winners and former champion Sydney apprentice Winona Costin has overcome a string of injury setbacks to make her mark in and out of the city.

Michelle Payne's Cup win may have attracted the headlines but it didn't knock down the door for women jockeys in Melbourne. Linda Meech is winning more than her share with limited metropolitan opportunities, Katelyn Mallyon is a shining light among the younger riders but there are not many more making their mark in the city. In Melbourne and Sydney, 'limited' is the key word, with the most utilised woman getting about a third the rides of most men on the top-twenty lists.

The situation is better in Brisbane. While all jockeys were left in the wake of the barnstorming Jeff Lloyd in 2016–17, Tiffany Brooker, Alannah Fancourt, Rebecca Williams and former champion apprentice and regular contender Tegan Harrison all made the top-twenty list and look likely to stay there for some years to come.

Tasmania has come a long way since Bev Buckingham created history back in the nineties. Siggy Carr, who got her real break when she went to the South Australian Apprentice

Academy, is high on the Tasmanian premiership and Raquel Clark is rated one of the best young riders in Australia.

Darwin continues the tradition set by the late champion Simone Montgomerie, with women numbering five of the top ten riders. Felicia Bergstrand was a revelation in 2016–17, achieving a strike rate of around twenty percent, while Melanie Tyndall, Vanessa Arnott, Kate Brooks and Simone Altieri were also regular city winners.

Rachel Hunt commands a lot of rides in Canberra but few other women got opportunities, although Kayla Nisbett makes the most of them, while Perth just doesn't appear to have room for women riders at all. Since outstanding young jockey Lucy Warwick took a leave of absence to deal with personal issues, the Perth jockeys premiership has become an all-male list.

The shining light in the equality stakes remains South Australia. The deeds of Lindop, Kah and Finnegan, and the owners and trainers who support them, speak for themselves.

CHAPTER 7

# UNDER PRESSURE

If 1979 was the year that celebrated the breakthrough for women in Australian racing, the bleak fourteen months between August 2013 and October 2014 was the time to mourn and recognise the price too many paid for their work in the industry.

In just over a year, Australian racing lost four jockeys, all outstanding horsewomen, and families lost wives, daughters, mothers and sweethearts. The deaths of Simone Montgomerie, Desiree Gill, Carly-Mae Pye and Caitlin Forrest stunned the most hardened racegoer and had women and men around the country wiping away tears in disbelief.

Outstanding South Australian and Northern Territory rider Simone Montgomerie fell in the Fanny Bay home straight during the running of the Lightning Plate on Darwin Cup Day in August 2013. Even though her mount Rhiagrand was leading 200 metres from the finish when it baulked and unseated Montgomerie, it appeared an innocuous incident that involved no other runner. She suffered massive chest injuries and never regained consciousness.

Montgomerie became apprenticed in Adelaide in 2005 at the age of seventeen. Four years later, she moved to Darwin to be closer to her parents Lee-anne and trainer Peter, who prepared quality stayer On A Jeune to win a Geelong Cup and run third to the great Makybe Diva in the 2005 Melbourne Cup. She found work with Darwin trainer Gary Clark and quickly established herself as a leading rider in the Top End. Just days before her death, she won the 2012–2013 Darwin Jockeys Premiership.

Clark spoke of Montgomerie's great riding ability at the Coroner's Inquest into her death in 2014: 'If some of the adult male riders were having troubles with a horse, you know, I'd put her on just to show them up that she could handle them and they couldn't,' he said. 'She was very good.'

The inquest found Rhiagrand had baulked and tried to stop at the pedestrian crossing in the Fanny Bay straight and that 'not even the most gifted of riders, as Ms Montgomerie was, could stay seated' due to the horse's 'very exceptional and unexpected' behaviour. The crossing was later removed and the 2013 Darwin Cup was abandoned and never run.

Champion Gympie jockey Desiree Gill was at the top of her game when she came down in a race at the Sunshine Coast on 9 November 2013. She had won the previous two South-East Queensland Jockeys Premierships and ridden four winners at Bundaberg the week before. She was riding Celtic Ambition in fourth position when the pace slackened and the maiden galloper clipped the heels of the runner in front and crashed to the turf.

A week after her death, the Roma Turf Club in the district in which Gill grew up paid tribute to the prolific rider by renaming their feature race the Desiree Gill Memorial Roma Cup. Two days later, hundreds turned out at the Gympie Showgrounds for the funeral of the champion country rider. Jockeys Larry Cassidy, Jim Byrne, Michael Cahill, Damian Browne and Melbourne Cup winner Chris Munce were among those who formed a guard of honour at the service.

In paying tribute to Gill after the tragedy, Racing Queensland chief executive Darren Condon said the death of the 45-year-old left 'a big hole in the racing fraternity'.

'She has been so much more than a jockey up here,' he said. 'She has worked in the training of apprentices for the past decade, and the young riders called her Mum.'

Central Queensland rider Carly-Mae Pye died during a Rockhampton jumpout in October 2014. Her mount broke both its front legs in the gallop and speared the 26-year-old into the Callaghan Park track before rolling on her. The former champion equestrian, who had ridden 199 race winners since 2006, suffered severe head and chest injuries and was put into an induced coma and died the following day.

Condon had the thankless task once again of paying tribute to someone gone far too soon. He described Pye as a 'salt of the earth racing person' and that her death had left the whole of North Queensland, not just the racing industry, in a state of despair.

'Carly-Mae was a true champion of our sport who will be remembered as a brilliant horsewoman,' he said immediately after her death in hospital. 'The racing community is in mourning this evening.'

One day after Pye's death, tragedy struck again. It was another Cup day and in another open sprint before the feature race on the program, and Australian racing lost one of its emerging stars. Caitlin Forrest was leading the 1000 metre dash on Colla Voce when the gelding shattered a shoulder at full pace rounding the home turn, came down in front of the field and caused major carnage on Murray Bridge Cup Day in 2014.

Unlike the Simone Montgomerie fall, the Murray Bridge crash looked bad from the moment Colla Voce crashed to the turf and brought down El Prado Gold, Ethball and Barigan Boy. The scenes on the track resembled a battlefield and racegoers didn't know whether to look down the straight searching for more information on the casualties or turn away in despair.

The nineteen-year-old apprentice, who was making a huge impact on South Australian racing, was airlifted to the Royal Adelaide Hospital, but died later that night from catastrophic brain damage.

More than 1200 people turned out the following week at Morphettville Racecourse to farewell the young rider. Champion jockey Clare Lindop spoke at the service and remembered Forrest as 'a complete natural'.

'Caitlin had an aura about her, she made people smile,' Lindop said, adding that she had a work ethic to match her talent. 'She was full of energy and fun, the next young gun with the world at her feet.'

Indeed, Forrest appeared to have a huge career ahead. An absolute natural, she started riding at Port August in July 2013. She won her first race a month later at Roxby and one month after that, gained her first ride at the provincials for a Balaklava win. She was fast becoming a rising star at the celebrated South Australian Apprentice Academy and went on to win the 2013–14 South Australia Provincial and Country Apprentice of the Year Award in a season that netted forty-four winners, including seven metropolitan races.

SAJC training supervisor Bill Forrestal remembers the day as one of the saddest of his life: 'The impact was immense … She was with me and the other apprentices at the Academy the day before and then I was with her family and closest friends at the hospital when we were told she wasn't going to make it. I'll never get over that. A part of Caitlin Forrest will be with me till the day I die.

'I've been in the industry a long time but the deaths of Caitlin and Simone Montgomerie, who'd worked with me for three years before going to Darwin, were more devastating than I could have imagined. When Caitlin died, there were more than twenty apprentices in the system that had to be helped work through their grief. Some of these were just fifteen, sixteen and seventeen and had never experienced death in their life. The outpouring of grief at the Morphettville service just showed what an impact Caitlin had made in such a short time. She was a lovely girl and a remarkably gifted rider.'

Caitlin Forrest's fellow rider and friend Libby Hopwood, aboard Barigan Boy, was fortunate to escape with her life in the Murray Bridge race. Adrian Patterson and Justin Potter somehow escaped serious injury. Hopwood's injuries, however, were far more serious than early reports of a broken collarbone and possible concussion. She also suffered bleeding on the brain, a broken shoulder blade, fractured vertebrae and a punctured lung and spent weeks in hospital and months convalescing. Her riding career was over.

Hopwood tried valiantly to convince stewards and herself she was able to ride again in races but, after several attempts, the parties agreed it was best to call it a day. She had significant faults in balance and perception and went through serious mood swings and depression in the months that followed the fall. At that stage, she even stumbled on any pavements that were not perfectly even when she took her dogs for a walk.

'I don't remember anything,' she says. 'There's about three weeks missing but I'm not challenging it. I skipped remembering it and I skipped all the pain from the hospital and that might be the best part of it. The body was pretty much fine after a while, it was more my head, which affected balance, depth, perception and my peripheral vision.'

The postscript to Hopwood's ordeal resembled the mindset of the magazine stories on women riders of the fifties — just a lot meaner in spirit. Retired at twenty-nine, she endured social media attacks for the natural weight gain from not riding trackwork and tipping the scales on a daily basis. She has since worked within the racing media and, more recently, joined Sky Racing as a permanent presenter.

Hall of Fame trainer Lee Freedman embroiled himself in a controversy immediately after Forrest's death with an emotional appeal to improve safety for Australia's jockeys. The backlash to Freedman's statement was perhaps as much to do with the timing, with many believing it was inappropriate to talk of such things so soon after the deaths of Pye and Forrest while emotions ran so high. Whether Freedman, an undisputed master of his profession, was correct in his comment that 'jockeys have got to stop this macho-rubbish that you tighten them up as much as you can', it certainly had no bearing on either fatality. Neither jockey died as a result of any crowding. Freedman went on to suggest policing of horses needed to be improved.

'Trainers should not be allowed to make the decision as to whether a horse runs and then run the gauntlet of the ire of the stewards — and I know, I have been a trainer for thirty years,' Freedman added. 'I know what trainers are like from the top to the bottom — a lot will run a horse that is borderline because they feel they know the horse.'

Freedman received plenty of criticism for his strong words and the timing of them but the comments drove home just how much the racing fraternity was hurting because of the deaths. While he did not point to a gender issue, many others did.

In the UK's Injured Jockeys Fund Report of early 2016, it was determined women were four times more likely to incur concussion than male riders. Debate has continued since over whether this is a matter of physiology or that fact that women, in many parts of the world but perhaps more often in Britain, were often forced to take rides on inferior horses, including those that acted up.

Race riding is widely regarded as one of the most dangerous occupations in the world. Since that devastating fourteen months, there have been more fatalities, including the death of mother-of-three Rebecca Black at Gore in

New Zealand in late 2016. Another young woman, Ashlee Mundee, had died in a race fall at Kunow in 2012 but the Kiwis, who have lost male riders during the past decade, were not making it a gender argument.

Nor was Australian Jockeys Association chief executive Paul Innes, responding to the debate after the spate of fatalities back in 2014: 'I don't believe the female factor has any bearing,' he said. 'There is no evidence to indicate that the recent tragedies are anything but accidents.'

National Jockeys Trust manager Tony Crisafi refused to be drawn into the gender debate: 'Let me just say we have some outstanding woman riders in this country,' he said. 'They make up twenty-seven percent of all jockeys and female apprentices represent between fifty-five and sixty percent of all new riders. Without women, we'd struggle to have a jockey base.'

More than 800 jockeys have died on Australian racetracks since racing records were first kept. It's a shocking, barely believable statistic. For obvious reasons, men make up the overwhelming percentage of these fatalities. They are the same reasons women, sadly, are now adding to the numbers.

CHAPTER 8

# TRACK BIAS

The men of the Australian Jockey Club were permitted to 'bring one female' into the grandstand in 1913. It's an outdated concept with wording that suggested the females were some sort of possession. But it was a time before the world had gone to war even once, when women had barely claimed their right to vote and were not about to infiltrate the male stronghold of the Australian racetrack. Surely after one or even two World Wars, things would improve for women? Not immediately. By the early seventies, there was still an actual white line within the Flemington Member's Enclosure directing where women could and could not go. They were strictly prohibited from crossing that line.

In 1978, women were still not permitted to become full members of the AJC. The principal club moved that the word 'male' be inserted before 'persons' to change the rules so women could not become full members of the AJC.

If women like Michelle Payne and Pam O'Neill have reacted with cynicism to the rules traditionally set by men and the continuation of a male mindset, perhaps these slices of history will explain it. The views of men within race clubs and the media and on the training track may have fuelled it further.

Legendary Melbourne trainer James Scobie conceded in the first half of the twentieth century that women might be capable of training quiet horses. Even in the late seventies, the great Bart Cummings said 'the AJC must be mad, women should not be competing in races against men'. In the same newspaper report, young champion jockey Malcolm Johnston said, 'they'd be better off in the kitchen'.

It may have seemed a ridiculous statement for Cummings to make but the man widely regarded as a racing genius came around years later. He even put Michelle Payne on one of his horses, Allez Wonder, to win the Group 1 Toorak Handicap in 2009. Johnston copped plenty of criticism for his particularly outdated and antagonistic view but was eventually able to swallow his pride and laugh about it in that *Racetrack Magazine* cover shot.

The male-dominated media largely dismissed women riders when the push was on for their acceptance in the seventies. *Sporting Globe* doyen Rollo Roylance said women 'just don't measure up' as jockeys. In 1979, *Sydney Morning Herald* racing writer Bert Lillye went into greater detail in a couple of his many criticisms of women riders: 'Racing is very tight and competitive here, when the money is on,' he said. 'It's hell for leather and no place for a lady. I just don't think they would be strong enough. Very few women light enough to ride in races have the strength to pick up or control a horse knocked off balance. I have never been an advocate of women jockeys riding in competition against the males.'

In 1982, then leading bookmaker Bill Waterhouse said punters were unlikely to back women jockeys because of a perceived lack of strength: 'The professional gambler is most hesitant to back a woman because she doesn't have the necessary vigor when it comes to using the persuader at the end of a race. Racing is really a man's sport.'

Bookmaker turned racing journalist Ken Callender attracted plenty of opposition for his many criticisms of women jockeys: 'Maree Lyndon ... keeps reminding us she likes to be called a jockey and not a woman jockey,' he wrote in 1987. 'I think Maree should be grateful for the reference because being a woman has kept her bank manager at his adding machine.'

He went on to say that Lyndon was far and away the best woman jockey he had seen 'but not even close to being among the top ten jockeys in Sydney'.

The nature of the media coverage of women in racing was largely patronising as mainly newspapers cashed in on the novelty aspect. The *Sun-Herald* ran a column called 'A Woman's Choice', in which Margaret de Montfort nominated a horse to follow from each race — and it was almost always an outsider because apparently women didn't take their betting seriously. That same year, the same paper ran the headline: 'Going strong wasn't something Linda was doing at all'. It referred to the two horses ridden by Jones at Doomben on that famous visit to Australia, when both finished down the track. A week later, Jones recorded her historic Morphettville win on Northfleet and the paper gave it three sentences under a small sub-heading.

When newspapers ran stories about women in racing thirty-five and forty years ago, they always mentioned their gender. Dulcie Thompson was a jockette and Pam Tanana was a Brisbane girl rider. Even the women were not convinced of their place in the industry.

When the *SMH* ran a story on women riders in the mid-seventies, even jockey Anne Luwitz said women riding in races was 'nothing to do with women's lib and all that nonsense'. The story was illustrated with a photo of a young jockey fixing her makeup next to a horse. Around the same time, Lady Jockeys Association president Wendy Smith said 'women cannot compete favourably against men. Some women would ride as well as men but on the whole they are not as strong'.

Headlines would be considered satire by today's standards. 'And the jockey wore a pigtail' and 'The woman is a jockey — and an air hostess' may be amusing now but they stopped women being taken seriously at the time. The support was, at best, half-hearted, with a New South Wales Trainers Associations spokesman saying women riders were 'something we have to learn to live with, the laws of the land will not allow discrimination'.

Despite the setbacks, and a lack of serious support, women slowly overcame the biases in a range of areas. Women had been riding in the most gruelling of all races, the Aintree Grand National, from 1977 but were not considered strong enough for Australian flat racing. Jane Parson and Lesley Bellden became the first women jockeys to win races at Canterbury and Randwick, respectively, in 1983, thereby breaking through one of the great traditional male bases. In 1988, Doris Bishop became the first woman in Melbourne or Sydney to run for a major board position when she stood for the Sydney Turf Club committee. It seemed to be too long in the making, considering New South Wales Counsellor for Equal Opportunity Geoff Cahill criticised thoroughbred racing in 1978 with the observation: 'Without any consideration for ability, women are refused the license granted a male.'

Columnist Bill Casey wrote a comical piece called 'The pitfalls of betting on a lady jockey', where his fictitious characters suggested women would be better off in the kitchen and that they were unreliable because they were 'inclined to panic under strain'.

Renowned racing journalist Max Presnell was more sympathetic. In one column in the mid-eighties, he was scathing of male jockeys riding aggressively against colleague Carol Tucker, who was aboard one of the favourites in the feature Hall Mark Handicap at Randwick. He concluded that he hoped 'the language wasn't as severe as the tactics'.

Women trainers always attracted far less criticism than their riding counterparts but that was often largely because they were less visible. The huge success of the legendary Gai Waterhouse, regarded as one of the world's great trainers of either gender, might also have had something to do with it.

Read into it what you will but a curious 2012 decision to give the great Black Caviar her most unexpected award had echoes of the outdated, cringe-worthy photo opportunities of the seventies — and reflected a bias of another era. When it came time for Sydney's *Daily Telegraph* to name its Sportswoman of the Year, they couldn't find a woman who deserved it. Not a woman in any field of athletics, nor a woman of the racetrack. They gave a horse, not a woman, the award.

## CHAPTER 9

# CHANGE OF TACTICS

If there has been an unsubtle bias against women in Australian racing for more than a century, the verdict is still out on the best way to deal with it. Gai Waterhouse subscribes to the 'get on with it' philosophy and suggests you simply prove how well you can do your job. Michelle Payne was outspoken once she had the right forum. Other women have been more and less vitriolic at different stages of their fight for equality. Some women didn't bother fighting, they just started their own clubs and created their own racing adventure. The women in racing clubs and organisations have been embraced as supportive, charitable and hard-working groups, and dismissed by some as exclusive replicas of the members' rooms. Some women argue they are a throwback to another era. Others, men and women, consider them a harmless social distraction that raise awareness of matters often overlooked.

The one thing that cannot be disputed is the awareness they have created for women who may have otherwise been lost to racing and, in many instances, the funds they raise for a raft of causes within the racing and equine industries.

The subject of women-only racing groups and syndicates generates controversy on either side of the gender debate. The meeting of social groups and clubs restricted to women is really only the business of those who attend it, many would argue, but whether it's legal to form syndicates where men are banned is another matter. Payne's 2016 launch of racing syndicates where only women could join was met with a mixed reception but it's unlikely the ethics or legality will ever be challenged. Certainly, if Chris Waller or David Hayes announced syndicates where women couldn't join, they would never see the light of day.

In a sport and industry that traditionally excluded women and has since been dragged, in some cases unwillingly, into the modern era, groups like the Carbine Club, Women in Racing and Ladies in Racing were among the best opportunities for women to get a foothold and become part of racing. Rather than being an outdated concept, the groups have flourished in recent years, brought more women into racing while providing a social outlet, introduced new owners to the game and raised money for many causes that would have otherwise been overlooked.

The Victorian Wakeful Club was formed in 2001 by a group of women who wanted to network and get involved in all aspects of the industry while maintaining a social base. Named after the legendary turn of the twentieth century mare Wakeful, the club's mission statement promoted bringing 'women together in a social atmosphere allowing them to be involved in their particular areas of interest'.

President Jenny Moodie says the Wakeful Club is a staunch supporter of several charities as well as students taking on equine studies. By 2017, it had eighty-nine full and associate members, including breeders, trainers and administrators.

'The Wakeful Club has offered annual scholarships to the National Centre for Equine Education and Melbourne Polytechnic and recently established the Victorian Wakeful Club Apprentice Jockey Training Program Scholarship to improve the skills of a nominated young woman rider,' she says. 'We are also strong supporters of the Lady in Racing Award, which was established by Wakeful founder Marie McCullough and Marcia Hill in 1993 to recognise the achievements and contributions of women in the thoroughbred racing and breeding industry and to encourage further involvement of women in the industry.'

Completely independent and separate to the Victorian body, the Tasmanian Wakeful Club also promotes women in racing under the name of one of Australia's all-time greatest horses. It was formed in 1997 to encourage networking and participation among women in racing and to bring more women into the industry. Its biggest events include the Hobart Cup Day luncheon and the Can Teen Tasmania Race Day, when it raises funds for the charity.

Women in Thoroughbred Racing Northern Territory (WTRNT) doesn't have the same easy-to-remember title but it's been thriving since it was formed in 2010. The non-profit organisation was also launched on a mission statement of female involvement, fundraising and social engagement.

'To promote and foster the ongoing conclusion of Women in the Thoroughbred Racing Industry throughout the Northern Territory,' the statement read. It also pledged to 'establish, maintain and conduct an association of non-political character' while running fundraising events to be honoured by 'persons of distinction' but importantly also to provide a voice for women in racing. To that end, it has clearly succeeded.

'The seed was planted in July 2009 over lunch and a glass of wine or two at Char Restaurant and now we have a committee of ten women connected to the racing industry and a growing financial membership base of 120,' president Michelle Graham says.

'Our overall aim is to raise funds to support the women of racing in the Northern Territory — the women that make it all happen, the women of Stable Street. Whether it's trainers, jockeys, apprentices, strappers, stable hands or trackwork riders, we aim to help women in the industry achieve their goals.'

WTRNT has taken a foothold in the Top End, with events held every two months as well as the annual Darwin Cup Carnival Luncheon which attracts around 200 guests each year. It receives plenty of industry support and the backing of the Darwin Turf Club, while in turn supporting the National Jockey Trust, Riding for the Disabled, Simone Montgomerie Fund and Taminim College. It also presents annual awards in a range of areas including Darwin and Alice Springs female trainer, jockey and apprentice awards.

The Women in Racing Group on the Gold Coast has an impressive slogan: 'Get Up, Get Dressed, Go Racing'. It captures plenty of media attention once a year at least, when it hosts the annual WIR Magic Millions Luncheon. It's one of a host of functions throughout the year designed to raise awareness of women in racing roles, support them where possible and also raise money for a list of racing and non-racing causes.

CHAPTER 10

# REVIEWING THE FORM

Australian racing has its fair share of women journalists, writers and presenters but you wouldn't have seen many of their names under the carnival headlines in the daily papers or on the weekly tipping charts over the years. Most have had to work hard to make a living freelancing or they've started their own ventures. Or they've moved overseas. It's not that they can't write or tip winners but is it that they haven't had the opportunities or haven't pursued them?

While Jo McKinnon's work as an anchor with Sky Racing opened the door for more women as presenters and Bronwyn Farr was a staple for readers of the industry-leading *Racetrack Magazine* in the nineties, the decades of Shelley Hancox writing for *The Age* hardly resulted in an influx of female racing writers on the dailies.

The women of the Australian racing media, even if most are not always found alongside the men in the press rooms, have earned their stripes. They know their racing and they have interesting views — and not at all the same views — on where it's been and which direction it needs to take.

**Kristen Manning** started out her journalism career in regular fashion as a cadet, working at *The Truth* newspaper in the mid-nineties but she always sought the freedom freelancing offered. By the end of her cadetship, she had become something of a breeding expert, knew how to write a good racing story and had a lot of contacts, so she pursued her dream to work for herself. By 1998, she was a regular stringer for *Winning Post* and the *Bluebloods* breeding magazine and picked up plenty of other jobs along the way.

'All I ever wanted to do was go freelance so I spent my cadetship making contacts and I've been freelance ever since,' she recalls. 'While I was at *Truth*, I did a few mating plans so I always thought I'd like to do that professionally. A few years later, Terry O'Sullivan became my first client when he got me to do a mating plan and that horse, Tails of Triomphe, went on to win a Group 1, the South Australian Derby. He told his clients, the word of mouth spread, and I was away.

'I think I was the first female racing cadet at *Truth* but I had a boss who didn't really care about gender so I was lucky there. You still get the occasional sexist rubbish on social media. I've had a few bad social media experiences, a few people who troll you, but I think I've learned how to deal with that now.'

Manning says racing clubs and administrators, rather than the media, need to move forward in their thinking towards women and men who are not part of the establishment.

'There are areas of racing that are very much a boys' club and not just that, a wealthy boys' club,' she says. 'I was speaking to a female stud owner recently who said she finds it hard at sales sometimes because they come up to her and ask where the man is.

'I think sexism in racing is there still but it's generally not in your face. There are probably freelance jobs I haven't got because I'm female but then I'd never know. I've found if you're on the outer with certain racing bodies, you can be in the wilderness but I'm pretty sure that's not just a gender thing.

'In my experience, one major body doesn't like female opinions. I want to see more women in admin. Racing needs to stop being afraid of women with a voice. Traditionally, race clubs and organisations around Australia have only wanted women who can organise fashion parades and I think they're only now starting to come to terms with women with a voice.

'One of the most ridiculous things in racing is wheeling out female models for the big trophy presentations. It sends a message that this is where we think a women's place is — looking pretty, saying nothing while men do the real job. It's how you market racing to the world and that's how it looks — women in their place. It has to go: it's so 1970s. You almost expect to hear Benny Hill music playing.'

Arguably the best-known face of women in the Australian racing media, **Jo McKinnon** has worked across all fields here and abroad for more than twenty years. A competition equestrian rider from an early age, she started out doing the police and other rounds as a cadet journalist for the *Herald Sun* before working her way into racing and then made the move to television when Channel Ten offered her a rare opportunity for the late-nineties: female sports reporter. It was the start of a glittering career on both sides of the camera, taking her to Sky Racing as its first female anchor and later host of *Racing Retro*, producer of the station's *Bred to Win* program before working for a couple of years in Hong Kong as a presenter and commentator. In between these jobs, she held executive roles with the Moonee Valley Racing Club and Aushorse and now runs her own media business and produces racing documentaries like the highly-rated *A Racetrack Somewhere.*

'I started in the days when they had the PM edition of the *Herald Sun* and I got thrown in the deep end covering trackwork at Flemington and Caulfield while Tony Meaney, a very respected racing journo was on leave,' she recalls 'That's where the real passion was ignited.

'I then went to Channel Ten, which was very exciting because the network had the racing rights back then. One of my jobs was to do a racing segment for *Sports Tonight* so once a week I'd go out to the track and do a preview of the weekend's racing and interview all the trainers. I also regularly interviewed the track watcher, the late Gavin Spain, and he taught me so much.

'Sky had approached me a couple of times before I agreed to join because I was happy at Ten and got to cover a range of sports as well as racing. But Sky wanted a female presence and eventually the lure of working full-time on racing was too much to reject.'

While McKinnon doesn't recall any obvious gender bias at any stage of her media career, she admits to feeling limited in how far she could go in the corporate world.

'I felt like racing to me was a comfort zone after doing general sport,' she says. 'Women doing sport's reporting on commercial TV was a real novelty but racing, perhaps because of my knowledge of the horse and my love of horse racing, I've always felt accepted in racing.

'There were a few moments when I started at Sky where a few viewers didn't like the fact I was a woman. I remember this one hand-written fax saying what would she know, she's a woman, get her off, and I was devastated. I look back and laugh now. But everyone gets negative feedback in racing and certainly the workplace was always good.

'When I worked at Moonee Valley, I harboured desires (still do to be honest) to run a major racing club in Australia. But I also have felt that it was going to be tougher to get there as a woman. There's never been a female CEO yet of a major racing body in Australia.

'The race clubs being run by women are the small, grass-roots clubs that need people to do bloody hard work and these women do that. There's some incredible women in racing administration, keeping the sport alive in remote communities but it's not translating to the top end of town.'

Sydney author **Jessica Owers** spent time as a child in Ireland and Scotland, has been writing for racing and breeding magazines all her adult life and was the Australian contributor to New York's *Thoroughbred Racing Commentary*. When she wasn't tracking down stories, interviewing people all over the country and then filing for the international website, she was beginning to research a book that became an award winner — *Peter Pan: The Forgotten Story of Phar Lap's Successor*. The book on the great stayer of the early thirties was so well-received, publisher Random House commissioned another and Owers produced *Shannon*, the story of the legendary 1940s galloper.

It was an unlikely choice for a young journalist immersed in modern horse racing to write two books on champions from seventy and eighty years ago but Owers brought their stories to life. The passion she had for the accounts of the two champions comes through in her views on all aspects of the industry.

'These days I consider myself more a racing author than a racing journalist,' she says. 'I grew up reading the Black Stallion books and the Saddle Club. I learned about Phar Lap and that led me to learn about Peter Pan, who was just an amazing animal. I love history and I love the opportunity to write about a subject and be immersed in the era. Narrowing a subject down to a few hundred words for beat journalism didn't appeal to me. Being able to write feature length stories always has. It's such a shame a lot of the magazines are gone now. And that's where all the online stuff has gone — to the detriment of correct writing.'

While Owers believes racing often plays to favourites, she says the days of women being held back because of gender are disappearing. As a freelance feature writer and journalist, she says she did not experience direct biases.

'I tend to think it's not so much a gender issue in racing, rather that racing can be very cliquey for men and women who don't have the right connections,' she says. 'Racing is full of big egos and I've found that, if you're a reed that bends in the wind, you do better. Since that Melbourne Cup win, perhaps Michelle Payne is paying the price for coming out and saying things that have rubbed a lot of people up the wrong way.

'I thought the way everyone went on about her for so long because she was a woman bordered on the ridiculous. She's a jockey who rode a great race to win. I thought by celebrating it so much based on her gender, we were actually regressing.'

**Jenny Chapman** has a great eye for a horse and she's not a bad tipster either. The Victorian-born television racing journalist, one of the world's best, doesn't make her living here though. She's been brought back a few times for expert comments at racing carnivals but she works full-time in Hong Kong.

When Chapman runs through the horses in the saddling enclosure at Sha Tin or Happy Valley, she does something most analysts fail to do — she judges them on way they look. Simple as that. Regardless of her early tip for the race, her best from the yard is simply the best looking horse from the yard. Not because it's favourite and not because it may have won its past three starts. Chapman knows if a horse is ready and those who subscribe to PayTV should listen.

Born in Mordialloc, Chapman was introduced to racing at a young age when her father Kel trained horses at Mentone. She could ride from as early as she remembers and, when the family moved to Caulfield when she was ten years old, she was riding trackwork and attending the local pony club. She got her license to ride in 'ladies' races at seventeen and rode competitively for the next ten years. Fair to say she knows how to handle a horse.

A former champion amateur rider in Victoria, Chapman has worked for the Seven and Ten networks in Australia but these days she's a paddock and form analyst in Hong Kong. So why isn't she still working in Australia?

'I fell in love with Hong Kong after I visited there a couple of times in the late seventies and I was always keen to live there at some stage,' she recalls. 'It started when my Dad sold the odd horse to Hong Kong. My husband, David [Price] and I went on a holiday there twenty-four years ago and decided to pack up and give it a go on the punt there. David was able to get employment through a local bloodstock agent and I was soon working for cable TV doing a racing preview and review show before being employed by the HKJC as a commentator.

'David and I could see that a lot of Hong Kong racehorse owners were being ripped off with bad purchases, so we decided to start our own bloodstock company, with the view to send the very best we could there. It paid off big time when superstar Silent Witness won his first seventeen starts and was crowned the fastest horse in the world.

'There are so many women who love the racing industry. In Hong Kong, there are a lot of women horse owners. It used to be a very male-dominated domain but not anymore.'

While Chapman chose to work abroad, the decision had very little to do with opportunities in Australia: 'I was always conscious that I was working in a male-dominated industry but I'd been working in it all my life anyway,' she says. 'I knew everyone in the business and I didn't experience any real issues with it.'

**Shelley Hancox** started her own syndication business almost thirty years ago while working for *The Age* and she's since put almost 10,000 people into a share of a racehorse. The doyen of Australian women racing journalists started on the broadsheet in 1968 before working for the *London Sun* in the early seventies and then returned to add commentary on Radio 3UZ (now Sport 927) and 3DB to her portfolio. Hancox believes there haven't been enough women in the business but is far from convinced it's a matter of any male bias.

'I was the first woman to work in racing on a proper newspaper and while *The Age* employed a couple more a few years later, they only stayed in racing for a year or two,' she recalls. 'I've been surprised more women haven't been involved in racing media. I don't think there's a bias though, I just think they haven't been interested. I can hardly ever remember seeing an ad for a racing journalist so maybe men have heard about the jobs through their contacts and are more likely to knock on the door. I went doorknocking at newspapers to get my foot in the door and I got it.'

Hancox says the fact women have held important jobs in regional racing clubs in decades gone by indicates the opportunities are there for those who have the interest.

'Yvonne Blackwood was the chief executive of Cranbourne Turf Club for years,' she says. 'Robin Levett was president at Kilmore and Helen Cantwell was secretary at Sale for a long time. These were women who worked in male-dominated areas and provided great service to racing.

'It's disappointing there haven't been more women in a lot of areas, including bloodstock. It's not that it's any old boys' club. Fifty percent of the people who buy a share in our horses are women so the interest is there. We have hundreds of women owners. Perhaps it's not a lack of interest, it's that not enough women look at racing as a profession.'

Hancox Bloodstock reports buying $6.2 million in horses for a racetrack return of around $17 million. That's a decent profit on what its principal calls a 'low outlay' on often bargain buy horses like Group 1 Goodwood Handicap winner, Sword. It gets women into racing on an equal footing with men and now Hancox believes it's up to them to take the next step.

When **Cathryn Meredith** isn't producing the upmarket *Ladies In Racing* magazine from her Brisbane base, she is a highly successful advertising woman and coordinator of women in racing events.

Like so many women making their mark in Australian horse racing, Meredith has taken the tumbles and done the hard yards. Her glossy quarterly only tells part of the story of a woman who learned to ride by falling off stock horses, 'and getting back on again', in her teenage years and who loved racing from the first time she went with father Ron Williams to the track as a kid.

Meredith has been editing the magazine since 2007 but her entry to the game came years earlier. She started working as a freelance advertising consultant in the late eighties with a company called Magazine Art, which produced a series of *Great Races of the World* souvenir programs — from the Melbourne Cup to the Golden Slipper and Magic Millions in her own Queensland backyard to the US Triple Crown races, the Japan Cup and Auckland Cup. It gave her the perfect introduction to the promotion of racing and she's learned enough over the years to know it needs to get better in some areas.

'Women need to be acknowledged as an integral part of the growth of the racing industry,' the editor stresses. 'Wagering organisations need to embrace the female market more as their betting promotions are generally male-orientated and clubs need to promote themselves more to the female market.'

While there is still a disparity within the ranks in metropolitan racing, Meredith points to the increasing number of women working within country and provincial racing clubs around Australia as a positive trend. She believes several factors, including the number of female jockeys and a significant interest in women attending race meetings for social reasons, auger well for further growth.

'Michelle Payne's Melbourne Cup win was pivotal but there has also been an increase in women being placed in management positions within clubs,' she says. 'Without the ladies attending the races, racing would not be what it is today. The biggest increase of the past decade has been the increase in female jockeys but also I love hearing the stories of the amazing women within the industry and what they have achieved. Many work behind the scenes and I'm proud that our magazine has been able to tell their stories.'

Meredith says the number of women in racing groups around Australia has become so significant that it led her to rebrand the magazine almost five years after it started to set it apart.

'Our first issue was called *Australasian Women in Racing* but in December 2011 we decided to change the name to *Ladies in Racing* to avoid confusion with the many women's racing organisations across Australia,' she says. 'That gives you an idea of how strong the interest of women in racing has become. It's also very diverse. Our readers are chief executives, club secretaries and managers, jockeys, strappers, breeders, owners, stud managers, fashionistas and a lot of men as well.'

Women have overcome the traditional biases to make their mark in the racing media. It's a curious fact, though, that their views on which horse might actually win a race are rarely sought. One online racing guide lists nine tipsters and they're all men. In some cases, the men have significantly less experience than the likes of breeding and racing expert Caroline Searcy or on-air presenters Lizzie Jelfs, Nadia Horne, Jamie Rogers and Mary Collier. The media is changing from the newspaper tipping panel and 'horses to follow' to electronic and on-line variations but apparently, in Australia, they haven't worked out that women can tip and report as well as the men.

## CHAPTER 11

# BLINKERS ON

Not one state or territory racing body around Australia is run on a daily basis by a woman. There are no female chief executives and Thoroughbred Racing South Australia is the only state board across the nation with a woman at the helm.

Just fifteen percent of all racing board members around Australia are women. The day-to-day running of racing is even more biased, with women making up only eight percent of the executive teams in all states and territories.

What is most frightening, perhaps, is that these disturbing statistics come at a time when racing has actually made some advances towards equality. It's not an affirmative action argument, suggesting the imbalance needs to be addressed with a bias towards women. There's enough talent in the women who have been trainers, owners, breeders, worked in other areas of racing and been executives in the broader business community to suggest they don't need any help. They just don't need to be the hindrance that has been part of racing culture for too long.

It's not that women have never played a role in management or boards. Robin Levett was the first woman to be elected president of a major regional turf club at Kilmore and she was a respected breeder who won the 1965 Victoria Derby with Khalif. Before Gai Waterhouse, she was known as the 'first lady of racing' but her deeds, and those of a few to follow, have not translated to a new generation of women in major decision-making roles.

It has been estimated that forty percent of race clubs around Australia are run by women. That figure includes every country race club, from the once and twice a year venues to flourishing country clubs and the strong provincial clubs where hard work, one-on-one contact with the public and networking all play major roles in the everyday running of the operation. It doesn't include very many metropolitan clubs.

The websites for many of Australian racing bodies feature plenty of women — they are usually young, vibrant and dressed in the most expensive outfits. The clubs have worked out the value of appealing to women, particularly for their major carnivals and social events, but haven't quite worked out the value of actually having women help run the show. A review of the state bodies makes compelling and often curious reading. Some states are moving with the times, others look like a throwback to the fifties.

The Victoria Racing Club is a surprising exception, considering its traditional views over the years. Amanda Elliott started 2017 as Acting Chairman of the VRC but ascended to the permanent role within a month to become the first female Chair of the board in the VRC's 153-year history. She was only the second woman ever to be elected to the board in 2002. Today, Elliott heads a board that also comprises Judge Katherine Bourke, Elisa Robinson and Sophie Cornell, giving women four of the nine places.

One of Elliott's first jobs with the VRC was to quash suggestions in a Newscorp story that the Melbourne Cup was going to be moved from its traditional first Tuesday in November. It was an important statement to issue on the back of some questionable proposed and actual changes to major races around Australia — although perhaps defence of a great tradition was not the first statement sought by those women and men seeking cultural change.

Racing Victoria employs Grace Forbes, Melissa Weatherley, Jane Rogan and Anita Blokkeerus in important roles but only one woman, Chief Commercial Officer Jane Ballantyne, makes the cut for the six-person executive team. In the board room, the recent departure of Jodie Leonard leaves Prue Hayes and Alice Williams as the only women with a vote.

Chief Commercial Officer Peta Webster is the only woman on the nine person Melbourne Racing Club executive team and those numbers are replicated among the elected members. The club could once again only find room for one woman, Patricia Faulkner, on its nine-member Board of Directors.

Racing New South Wales has an eight-member racing board. Carole Molyneux-Richards and Saraane Cooke are the only women. Down the road, the Australian Turf Club employs twenty-two people in management roles — only two women make the cut, with Executive General Manager of Human Resources Jennifer Schembri the only one on the seven-person executive team.

Queensland, the state that did so much for the advancement of women riders, has an embarrassing level of female representation in the front office and boardroom. Racing Queensland's Thoroughbred Advisory Panel has twenty-one people on it. Not one woman. The Brisbane Racing Club has a four-person executive team and General Manager of Sales Katie Churchill is the only woman. As for the elected representatives, the BRC website features a photo of its Board of Directors: ten very well presented, well dressed people who look like they mean business. They're all men.

It gets considerably better in South Australia. The Thoroughbred Racing SA Board is chaired by Frances Nelson QC, who heads a seven-person panel that also has the services of former Gawler Jockey Club chairperson Judith Jones. While they are the only women on the board, their experience cannot be denied. Nelson is one of the major figures in the South Australian legal system and has been Chairman of the SA Parole Board for thirty-four years, while Jones spent ten years as chief executive of Barossa Council. In addition, Nelson is Deputy Chairperson of the Racing Australia Board but also the only woman on it. A woman also holds an important position on Racing Australia's executive team, with Jacqueline Stewart working as the Keeper of the Australian Stud Book.

The South Australian Jockey Club also recognises the value of having women on board, with Bodelle Francis recently appointed the permanent chair of the eight-member board. The story is not as strong in executive roles in the southern state, however, with TRSA's Michelle Greene and the SAJC's Emily Browne the only women on the senior management lists.

Out west, Paula Sullivan is the only woman on the eight-member Perth Racing Board and there is not one woman on the executive management team. Tasracing's four-person executive team is all men but there's a better balance on the Board of Directors, with Tania Price, Helen Galloway and Robyn Whishaw making up almost half of the seven members.

Thoroughbred Racing Northern Territory has all men on its seven-member Board but two women make it on to the Darwin Turf Club Board. With eleven members, there was certainly room for them.

While most forward-thinking people acknowledge management positions should be judged on the merits of the candidates and not gender, suggesting women should not be advantaged or disadvantaged, many racing bodies appear to be overlooking an important issue.

If race crowds are declining for weekly meetings, surely change needs to be made. If numbers are up for the big social and carnival days, and these crowds come about by appealing to women in mass advertising, why are the clubs and the promoters not doing the most basic marketing and math?

These are the facts:

The traditional model of attracting men to race meetings for the purpose of having a bet is a thing of the past.

Advertising aimed at women equals bigger crowds.

The men who once populated racetracks can now bet in a TAB, via the computer, over the phone or at other venues.

They can attend other sporting events.

The biggest race crowds attract a mix of women and men in a social environment.

Women run major companies around the world just as effectively as men.

This leads to an obvious question. When will race clubs take off the blinkers and recognise that women in important positions may actually bring a new perspective to the management and marketing of thoroughbred racing? Or are they already notifying a gear change?

Racing Victoria board member Prue Hayes certainly believes the changes are already being made in many areas. While there are still improvements to be made, she says racing is becoming more of a leader than a follower in equal opportunity.

'We've got more women in the executive roles at Racing Victoria than ever before,' she says. 'I've never felt any tokenism from my first day on the Racing Victoria Board, not even slightly. My opinion was valued and respected and I was given my time and my chance to be heard. I think the days of women being treated as tokens or not being given the opportunity is nearly a bygone era in the racing industry now.'

Nobody would question Hayes' credentials and that she's earned her stripes and the right to have her opinions considered. Married to Hall of Fame trainer David Hayes, she is General Manager of Lindsay Park Racing Stables, one of the world's great racing establishments with which she has been linked for more than twenty-five years.

'It could have been that women didn't apply for the senior positions as much as they should have but that is fast being corrected now,' she says. 'There are plenty of women applying for board and management positions and I'm sure you're going to see a lot more women making decisions in racing.

'I think the racing industry's actually pretty healthy as far as equality is going. The one area we need to improve on is getting more female owners. Even that is slowly improving. There are more women and families coming back to the races. We weren't able to sell our product well enough to show the horse as the equine athlete and to show the real people behind the scenes. That's something that had to happen to get women to become more involved in the sport and industry, that it's not just a pastime for men having a bet.

'The encouraging thing for Victoria is that the person now in charge of seeing that advertising aimed at getting more women into the industry and to the track is a woman. But I think we have to encourage female involvement at all levels. We administrators have it easy at times, the women and the men I really admire are those that get up at four o'clock every morning and do the hard work.'

Changes can be seen in some areas, if not others. The speed of the change is the argument. Katie Page is co-owner of Magic Millions. Beryl White bred more than 350 horses including thirteen Group 1 winners with her late husband Geoff and was one of Australia's great owners. Elliott, Nelson and Frances are in charge of important racing boards. Jane Ballantyne is a major force in forging future marketing directions for Racing Victoria.

Perhaps, as Shelley Hancox says, more women need to follow these leads and push hard to increase female participation at the higher levels within the industry.

Page, also chief executive of Harvey Norman, in 2014 launched a Magic Millions Racing Women campaign aimed at encouraging more women into the racing industry and racing ownership. She questioned why less than twenty-five percent of racehorse owners are women and, more importantly, why an even lower percentage have decision-making roles within the industry.

Racing Victoria proudly announced in 2014 that female participation in racing had increased substantially over the previous ten years. The percentage of jockeys had risen from ten to twenty-two percent, trainers were up from nineteen to twenty-four percent and forty-one percent of Victorian race clubs were managed by women. The numbers were looking good but what the statistics didn't say is that not many of the women riders or trainers were getting opportunities in the city and most of the race clubs run by women were regional ones.

## CHAPTER 12

# TURNING FOR HOME

*Racing for the Future,* Racing Victoria's strategic plan for 2013–2016, said all the right things about inclusion and promoting women in racing. The twenty-four-page manifesto related to all aspects of Victorian racing — the people, the horses, the turnover and the integrity.

Amid a series of glossy photos, including a curious pic of Hong Kong star Military Attack at Sha Tin, is a full-page image of a glamorous young woman cheering at the races. Glamorous young women have long been a part of the promotion of racing, and the document dedicated several paragraphs to promise women would also be considered part of the industry going forward. Three years after that, Michelle Payne for one certainly didn't believe the promise was being delivered.

In what have become the most famous words ever spoken by an Australian sportswoman, Payne's outburst after winning the 2015 Melbourne Cup aboard rank outsider Prince of Penzance was heard around the sporting world.

'It's such a chauvinistic sport,' she said soon after unsaddling. 'I'm so glad to win the Melbourne Cup and hopefully it will help female jockeys from now on to get more of a go because I believe we don't get enough of a go.'

Of course, Payne went on to make her famous 'everyone else can get stuffed' comment about owners not considering women for rides. Debate can go back and forth over the right of an owner to choose whomever he or she wants on their horse but the main focus of Payne's controversial comments were the charge that women weren't getting a fair go.

So what were Victoria and New South Wales, two of the most important racing regions in the world, doing to redress the balance and sort out more than a century of bias?

These were the two states that ought to have been leading the way from the start but followed some way behind Queensland and South Australia. They make up more than half the county's population and, more significantly, are where most of Australia's greatest races are run. If the homes of the Melbourne Cup, Caulfield Cup, Cox Plate, Golden Slipper and Victoria and Australian Derbies were not going to embrace change, women would struggle to be taken seriously.

In 2013, *Racing for the Future* said RV would 'grow female participation and interest in racing and strive to become an Australian sporting leader in gender equality'. It said it would 'capitalise on the relatively higher levels of female engagement in our sport by seeking to boost female participation (from jockeys, trainers and stable hands to owners and administrators)'.

It hasn't yet. Women are on boards and in executive

positions but the percentages remain low; on an average Saturday metropolitan race card in Melbourne, about ninety-five percent of the riders are men and there are even meetings where not one woman is riding. Not even Michelle Payne.

It seems Payne's comments immediately following the great race overshadowed one of the great rides of the modern era. Her Melbourne Cup performance lost nothing in comparison to the deeds of Brett Prebble on Green Moon in 2012 or John Letts on Beldale Ball in 1980. They stand out as two of the most astonishing rides in modern Cup history and surely the difference between winning and losing; so was Payne's ride. Despite the effort and the headlines, owners have not been clamouring to engage a jockey who showed she can be the difference between winning and losing.

Perhaps they will take more kindly to Katelyn Mallyon, just out of apprentice ranks and already proving herself one of the best young jockeys in the country. Granddaughter of multiple Group 1 winning jockey Mick Mallyon, she is a dual Victorian Apprentice of the Year. She was the first female to win the title in 2011–12, then spent much of the following season sidelined after a serious fall which resulted in her being put into an induced coma but she returned to claim the title again in 2013–14.

In 2016, top Tasmanian jockey Raquel Clark was denied a permit to ride in Melbourne despite being highly placed on her state's premiership list. The reason given was that she did not have enough experience riding in city races — notwithstanding that Hobart is a city. It didn't stop the young gun riding with polish and winning at her first visit to the very tricky 'metropolitan' South Australian course of Oakbank some months later and backing it up with more success the following week at Morphettville.

Many male jockeys had not been prevented from riding in Melbourne without significant metropolitan experience over the years. The stance bewildered Australian Jockeys Association chief executive Des O'Keefe, who observed that the criteria the jockey didn't meet was 'very, very odd'. Clark, who was denied the 2015–16 Tasmanian jockeys premiership after being injured in a fall at Spreyton, was rated a B-grade rider in Victoria and stewards said she needed to prove herself on the provincial circuit first.

More worrying for Victoria than the plight of female jockeys is the absence of women on trainers' lists. There's not a woman at the high end of either the metropolitan or state-wide premierships, with Cindy Alderson, Gwenda Johnstone and Wendy Kelly regular winners in the country but only able to pick up the occasional city race.

Racing Victoria insists it is being very proactive in bringing women into the racing industry. It has created a strategic framework, diversity and inclusion strategy, women's mentoring programs and a project called 'No Barriers, No Limits!'.

The framework talks about the key enablers of talent and diversity as it strives to 'have the best people managing our sport from a diverse range of backgrounds and with a diverse range of skills'. The bottom line is that RV is chasing gender and cultural diversity and that it recognises 'the need to better reflect the community in which we operate and which is largely split fifty–fifty males and females'.

The Diversity and Inclusion Strategy was launched in 2015 and achievements so far include a prayer room and lactation facility, flexible working arrangements and a domestic violence support policy. It is now in 'phase two'.

RV and Tabcorp have joined forces on the women's mentoring program, which recognises that 'focusing on the development of women, organisations can better utilise their talent pool'. Who would have imagined?

No Barriers, No Limits! has a goal of increasing female participation across the industry and 'to understand current trends' as well as potential barriers and opportunities. It is overseen by a steering committee comprising executives from RV, Country Racing Victoria, the Australian Trainers Association and the Victorian Jockeys' Association. RV says the aim of the project is to increase long-term contributions from women, with pilot groups gathering information on diversity and inclusion at the industry level.

Racing Victoria's mindset is commendable but there seem to be a lot of programs, initiatives and strategies aimed at one very simple principle. Treat everyone fairly. Linda Meech doesn't need frameworks or strategies to ride in races but, despite her outstanding record, she doesn't get a lot of rides at metropolitan Saturday meetings.

RV People and Culture Manager Anita Blokkeerus believes that while there still need to be changes in attitude before even the best women jockeys are always considered on their merits by owners and trainers, significant positive changes are being made across the industry. Perhaps having a manager to deal with people and culture is a start.

'We have a highly valued and talented team of female

employees at RV who all make an important contribution to both the organisation and industry,' she says. 'RV also manages the State's raceday officials such as clerks of course, clerks of scale, judges and barrier attendants and this is an area which we have identified with the potential to further grow the number of women employed as they are currently low in comparison to other areas of our workforce.'

Blokkeerus cites an upward trend in figures for both women jockeys and trainers as an encouraging sign for the years ahead: 'Data from the first half of the 2016–17 racing season shows that twenty percent of active trainers in Victoria are female,' she says. 'RV introduced a dual license in 2016, allowing jockeys to take on a restricted trainer's license. Of the seven trainer–jockey licenses to be granted, six have been to women including Michelle Payne, Linda Meech and Jackie Beriman who are taking the opportunity to broaden their careers.

'In the first half of the 2016–17 season, we've seen the percentage of active jockeys in Victoria that are female grow from 20.5 to 24.2 percent [so] not surprisingly the number of rides by female jockeys rose significantly during this period. That has not yet translated into genuine increases within our metropolitan riding ranks, but with females currently representing forty-five percent of the apprentice jockeys based in Victoria, we expect that an upward trend will evolve over time due to the volume of participation.

'The decision to engage a jockey is ultimately that of the owners and trainers and not Racing Victoria. There has been an attitudinal change over recent decades to the engagement of female riders, although it is fair to say that we do require further acceptance from owners and trainers to accelerate that trend on our metropolitan tracks. RV's role is to ensure that we are investing in the development of young female riders via our Apprentice Jockey Training Program to ensure they are equipped with the skills to earn those opportunities on merit.'

Blokkeerus is hopeful about the future for women in Victorian horse racing. She expects greater diversity in the years to come and suggests the trend has already started.

'We have set targets in terms of female engagement at the board level and it has been pleasing to have [had] three female directors working to guide the organisation and industry throughout the past year,' she adds. 'The composition of the board is open to change, with amendments to the RV Constitution — which will transfer the appointment of the Board from the industry to the Minister for Racing. Our expectation is that diversity will remain an important component of the appointment process.'

In New South Wales, trendsetting trainers Betty Lane, Gai Waterhouse, Barbara Joseph and Gwenda Markwell all took control of their own situations. They didn't wait for initiatives and they were hardly granted their opportunities.

These days, Waterhouse is one of the few women trainers to have an influence in the Harbour City. With the exception of Waterhouse and Perth's Alana Williams, the lack of presence of significant women in Australian metropolitan training ranks looks like a throwback to the seventies.

Women may have been allowed to train for more than forty years but someone forgot to tell them or the owners who would be employing them. Only two women feature in the top-ten list of trainers in the five major Australian capitals and they both share the role with men — even the legendary Waterhouse. Alana and husband Grant Williams have made a serious impact on Western Australian racing and are the reigning Perth champion training combination; Waterhouse has promoted Adrian Bott from within the stable ranks so she can devote more time on the ground to the actual training of the horses.

As for the other metropolitan lists, they may as well be a men's club. Women virtually don't rate a mention in Adelaide, though Sue Jaensch and Nicole Bruggemann regularly feature high on the country circuit. Desleigh Forster is the only woman to have made a significant impact in Brisbane in recent years, but Kelly Doughty does well on the Gold Coast — where Helen Page has become something of a legend — and Krystle Johnston and Denise Ballard get a lot of country winners.

Veteran horsewoman Barbara Joseph, in partnership with Paul Jones, continues to make her presence felt in Canberra, Kerry Petrick has been a genuine success story in Darwin and rising star Tegan Keys has an outstanding strike rate in Hobart but the major cities struggle to recognise or promote women trainers.

If owners, even male owners, are happy to put a woman on to ride and male trainers promote the woman jockeys, why are women trainers not being considered in the same light?

More than the manifestos and strategic plans, perhaps, it's been the deeds of a handful of outstanding riders that have demanded the nation's two largest states take women jockeys seriously.

Kathy O'Hara, half of that iconic Gosford dead-heat, was top New South Wales apprentice in 2005. When sister Tracey went to the country to continue her career, Kathy stayed in the boiler room of Sydney racing. Many doubted the decision to ride against world-class jockeys, some of whom were entrenched with massive stables, on a weekly basis. But Kathy was up for the fight.

Payne and Linda Meech are no longer allowed to ride in New South Wales and Queensland because of the policies within those states to ban trainer–jockey licenses. With women riders getting fewer opportunities than men, the dual license is seen by some as a viable way of continuing in the industry. While those states did not make the policy a gender issue, it affects women more than men because a greater percentage of women jockeys are likely to seek dual licenses to expand their opportunities.

'I don't need to ride in Sydney anyway so it doesn't really affect me at the moment,' Meech says. 'They set the rules and I guess it means that, unless I was to give away training, I won't be riding there again. It is a pity because I loved riding up there when I spent three or four years with Gai [Waterhouse] but that's their rules and I don't let it bother me.'

Racing NSW is on the record saying it would not amend the rules 'after receiving strong recommendation from its stewards on integrity issues associated with dual licenses'.

Integrity has become something of a buzz word in Australian racing. Was betting integrity challenged, if not compromised, when the first running of the 2017 Sydney Cup was called off mid-race while some of the best jockeys in the business continued on unaware? Was business integrity questioned when there was huge media attention for a rich new race that looked like a carbon copy of a race run earlier in the year in Florida? Both instances certainly attracted huge debate and some condemnation. Somehow, a jockey riding a horse he or she trains is considered unacceptable and an opportunity to address the changing demographic is lost.

The VRC, a rigid bastion of convention, is starting to take steps to recognise and embrace the change in the landscape. Before the history-making decision to appoint Amanda Elliott as its chairperson, it held an exhibition recognising women's contribution to racing at the Melbourne Sofitel in October 2016. The exhibition featured portraits by photographer Martin Reddy of nine women within the industry: Judge Natashia Radford, Clerk of the Course Remi Gray, saddler Sophie Clark, equine veterinarian Emma Wood, farrier Natasha May-Keas, cadet stipendiary stewards Samantha Davison, Stella Stevenson and Kirstie Vanderziel and stable manager and broadcaster Lizzie Jelfs.

'The VRC is excited to celebrate and recognise the valuable contribution of women in racing,' said the VRC's customer engagement head Caroline Ralphsmith. It's yet to be seen whether the exhibition reflects a new era of inclusion but the statement was well received.

A review of the boards, the executives and most significantly the race fields themselves, indicates that, for all the progress and posturing, women right now are minority stakeholders in Australian racing. The initiatives and strategies are carefully-worded and may eventually have an impact but the move is coming from a long way back. The race for women to be taken seriously may have turned for home but there's a long straight ahead.

## PART II

# A QUALITY FIELD

From the dawn racetrack to the breeding barn, the stable, the office and even the broadcasting booth and the judge's tower, women are contributing to the racing landscape like never before. There are still the forgotten individuals and there probably always will be — women scratching out a living working tirelessly with barely a day off, just as many unknown men have done before them. The numbers are growing at long last and, while there will always be battlers of either gender, at least women can now talk of their achievements and not just their dreams. The stories of the women who have had an impact on Australian racing would already make countless volumes. They can't all be told; here are a few of them.

Trainer

# GAI WATERHOUSE

In the late eighties and early nineties, one of the great debates over women's rights and recognition played out across the newspapers, television, radio talkback and in the male-dominated boardrooms of Australian racing while Gai Waterhouse went through an excruciating wait to be granted her trainer's license. This was the woman who had managed Tulloch Lodge, one of the world's great training businesses, while her legendary father Tommy (T. J.) Smith recuperated from a knee operation. This was the woman who could have given seminars to teach men all across the country how to prepare a horse to run at its best on race day. She wasn't the equal of the average male trainer, awaiting her chance to prove it, she was in a different league to most of them.

The wait came because she was married to bookmaker Robbie Waterhouse, one of the men warned off Australian racetracks for his role in the infamous 1984 Fine Cotton ring-in — when the talented Bold Personality raced as the moderate Fine Cotton in Brisbane. It was, and remains, one of the most serious crimes anyone can commit on a racecourse and Gai Waterhouse was being punished for her non-involvement in the scandal. Argument raged in courts, bars, TABs and homes as to whether a man would have been locked out for his wife's indiscretions. Eventually commonsense won out and Gai Waterhouse was granted a trainers' license. Nine years later, husband Robbie was granted a reprieve from an onerous life sentence and allowed back on the track. The couple's marriage held up through the tumult and thrived and eventually Robbie returned to bookmaking.

Waterhouse had a way with horses, knew how to promote a business that was respected around the world and learned from arguably one of the two greatest thoroughbred trainers this country has ever produced. Like Bart Cummings, T. J. Smith was a groundbreaking horse trainer and his accomplishments were revered by anyone around the world who knew their racing. He won thirty-three straight training premierships in the enormously competitive Sydney marketplace, trained two of the all-time greats in Tulloch and Kingston Town, won Australia's greatest races on multiple occasions including Melbourne Cups, Caulfield Cups, Cox Plates and thirty-five Derbies. His 'bone and muscle' training philosophy (one shared in a modified way by daughter Gai) was to run them if they were ready and his attitude towards racing the forward juveniles and collecting the riches while they were available, enabled him to win the world's greatest two-year-old race, the Golden Slipper, six times. His daughter equalled that record when champion colt Vancouver won the race in 2015.

The honour roll for Gai Waterhouse puts her amongst

Tracy and Kathy O'Hara create history by dead-heating at Gosford in 2005.
Photo: Bradley Photographers

*top*: Michelle Payne wins the 2015 Melbourne Cup aboard Prince of Penzance. Photo: Sharon Lee Chapman

*middle:* Michelle Payne holding Australian racing's greatest trophy. Photo: Sharon Lee Chapman

*bottom:* Katelyn Mallyon, Kayla Nisbet and Nikita McLean. Photo: Sharon Lee Chapman

*top:* Champion jockey Clare Lindop aboard Royal Rumble at Morphettville. Photo: Sharon Lee Chapman

*left:* Gai Waterhouse celebrates after creating history with Fiorente in 2013 as the first Australian woman to win the Melbourne Cup. Photo: Sharon Lee Chapman

*right:* Trailblazing racecaller Victoria Shaw. Photo: Sharon Lee Chapman

*left: Ladies in Racing* editor Cathryn Meredith. Photo courtesy of the author

*right:* Racing Victoria Judge Natashia Radford. Photo courtesy of the author

*bottom:* Gai Waterhouse and Star Thoroughbreds founder Denise Martin. Photo: Sharon Lee Chapman

*top:* Racing promoter Jennifer Bartels with legendary French trainer Criquette Head-Maarek. Photo courtesy of the author

*bottom:* Champion Victorian rider Linda Meech all strength winning at Sandown. Photo: Sharon Lee Chapman

*top:* Leon Macdonald and Clare Lindop — SA's best trainer-rider combination after one of their many wins. Photo: Sharon Lee Chapman

*left:* Hong Kong-based journalist Jenny Chapman and leading Hong Kong trainer Tony Cruz. Photo courtesy of the author

*right:* The Burnewang North team — Aaron and Emma Todd, Tanya Edwards and owner Cathy Hains. Photo courtesy of the author

*top:* Leading WA training partnership Alana and Grant Williams. Photo courtesy of the author

*middle:* Journalist and presenter Jo McKinnon in her Sky Racing days with John Singleton, Ron Dufficy and Richard Freedman. Photo courtesy of the author

*bottom:* Award-winning racing photographer Sharon Lee Chapman

*top:* Gai Waterhouse trains through the mist at Newmarket in England. Photo: Sharon Lee Chapman

*bottom:* The Women in Thoroughbred Racing Northern Territory (WTRNT) syndicate celebrates a Darwin win with training great Gai Waterhouse. Photo: DarwinRacingPhotos.com

the absolute greats of world racing. She sits third on the all-time list for Group 1 winners in Australia. She trained her first Group 1 winner when Te Akau Nick won the 1992 Metropolitan just nine months after getting her license and it took a saturated track and the first of the international invaders, Vintage Crop, to deny her a win in the following year's Melbourne Cup with the same horse. She was inducted into the Australian Racing Hall of Fame in 2007, after just fifteen years as a full-time trainer. She is, surely, the world's best woman trainer and one of the best regardless of gender.

Perhaps the wait made Waterhouse a better business trainer. She already knew how to prepare a racehorse but, when she was finally allowed to train in her own right, she brought a steely resolve with her to strive for perfection and results. What it didn't do was change her effervescent personality and she made sure she was always available to chat to the public, take any question from the media and stop for a photo with supporters or owners.

'It was very tough, they made it nearly impossible,' she recalls without any obvious animosity. 'It wasn't necessarily because I was a woman, I was married to someone who had been warned off.'

Such was the opposition to Waterhouse, despite her obvious and proven ability to train; the Australian Parliament had to intervene on anti-discrimination grounds and determined someone could not be denied a license based only on their marital status.

When the path was clear for her to finally train in her own right, Australian racing was given added impetus that no marketing firm could create. Gai Waterhouse, the arts graduate who had acted in Australian television soap operas and on the English stage, knew how to talk to people and get them interested in racing through her infectious energy. She was a whirlwind, winning races from the get-go, as though she wanted to prove to the doubters that her grounding from childhood and natural ability made her destined to become a great in her field.

'I was around the stables with my father for much of my life so it was a natural environment for me,' she says. 'When I came back from overseas, I wanted to make a career in racing and Dad was happy for me to join him and his brother Ernie in the stables. I found it fascinating, I found it always interesting, I found it very challenging and I was constantly learning. The days were long, I started early but it was great.'

For all she had achieved and learned from the training genius Tommy Smith, she was curiously unsure about whether she would make the grade on her own.

'No I did not at all think I would just immediately become a top trainer,' she recalls. 'I just enjoyed doing what I was doing. I enjoyed working and assisting my father. I did all his PR, I spoke with the owners, I communicated to them how their horses were going.

'I think I'm a very patient person, I think that's been my strength as a trainer. I see things in horses and I'm very accepting of their faults. Dad said after I won the second Doncaster with Pharaoh, who had been broken down, that he couldn't have won it. He said he wouldn't have been as patient. That meant a lot to me.

'I couldn't break Dad's record, I couldn't improve on it.

His record was extraordinary: there's no record in the world that matches his record. It's a one-off.'

Despite her patience, Waterhouse has always been quick to act when she sees an opportunity. It's patience mixed with energy and enthusiasm and, for the great trainer, the qualities are not mutually exclusive.

'When I got started, I did things very quickly,' she says. 'I made them happen. I didn't know how to run a stable but I must have had a knack about it.'

Knack might be an understatement. Waterhouse trained 100 Group 1 winners in the shortest time in Australian history, faster than even her father or Cummings. The first five horses she ever took to the racetrack won. The first horse she saddled for a Group race won and, more recently, the first time she started a horse in a jumps race, it won too.

With that many firsts, no wonder Gai Waterhouse is known as the First Lady of Australian Racing. Without doubt, she warrants even greater accolades than that. Her record with horses that are not supposed to win is outstanding and her ability to keep winning the world's greatest race for precocious juveniles is remarkable.

'The Golden Slipper is the most fantastic race because it has a certain sex appeal for Australia,' she says. 'It's the world's best two-year-old race and it's essential for the Australian breeding industry. Those horses like Pierro, Sebring, Danzero and Vancouver are really exciting horses. But the greatest thrill I got was when Ha Ha won the race in 2001. At first, I thought I'd just won the race — which is an amazing thrill in itself — and then realised I'd landed the trifecta [with Excellerator and Red Hannigan].'

Waterhouse finds it hard to name her greatest thrill in racing because there have been so many — Pharaoh's unlikely Doncaster win, the Golden Slipper trifecta, dealing with the massive expectation of taking the favourite into the 2013 Melbourne Cup.

'The Melbourne Cup was obviously a highlight after coming close a few times and I knew I had the horse to win when Fiorente lined up,' she says. 'Confident though? Well yes I was but there was a lot of pressure going into it because it is Australia's iconic race and it's so hard to win. And so many people were expecting me to win the race.

'It's hard to pick the best moment but the Cup comes close. I've loved training good horses to win good races, sometimes against the odds. I loved the weight-for-age champion All Our Mob, he had a lovely personality, but it's hard to pick your best or favourite horse. It's like asking you to name your favourite child. You love them all. They have characteristics you love, some have characteristics that drive you crazy but you still love them.'

Waterhouse considers managing to be a good mother to children Tom and Kate while building her training empire back in the early nineties is one of her greatest achievements. Through the turmoil of the Fine Cotton fallout and the delay in her trainer's license, she and Robbie stayed strong and gave the kids a close family upbringing. Tom went on to be a leading corporate bookmaker and Kate went into fashion and on to a career as a newspaper columnist.

'I think if you're a man, you can knock off and go home and then come back to work a bit easier with fewer family pressures,' Waterhouse says. 'A mother, on the other hand, is expected to look after the children or be involved with your husband and the kids. There's more pressure, I think, to make the marriage work, to help the kids grow up so they're not lunatics. You have to spread your time very carefully.'

Waterhouse believes in the rights of women to achieve whatever they can in thoroughbred racing but also believes it has to be hard-earned. Just as women were wrongly denied chances in years gone by, she doesn't want to see them being gifted opportunities simply because of their gender.

'I'm not so much into being granted equal opportunity, I think you make your opportunity,' she says. 'If they've got the will to do it or got the talent, there's no reason a male or female can't be a successful trainer or jockey these days.

'Australia has a little way to go in the workforce in its attitude towards women but it is improving all the time and so is racing. There aren't many women running major companies and I don't see enough in senior executive roles in racing, either. If we keep chipping away at the glass ceiling, it does crack. I don't judge jockeys on their gender. If they're good enough, I use them.'

Perhaps, or probably because, she's a woman, Gai Waterhouse has been the subject of speculation that she may be about to retire. Well, the good news for those of us who have marvelled at the great woman's racing knowhow for a couple of decades, is that rumours of her impending retirement are greatly exaggerated and perhaps a decade or two early. Waterhouse addresses the rumour, saying she'll give it as much time as it's worth: 'I've heard it. There's no strength to it.'

# Jockey

CLARE LINDOP

She's not a 'lady rider' and does not take well to being called a 'woman jockey' either. Clare Lindop is a jockey. A very good one at that. She has never asked for any concessions from her male colleagues or the racing public and it's an attitude that has paid off for her for more than twenty years. Three Adelaide metropolitan jockey premierships, four Group 1 wins from limited opportunities and more than 1300 winners are a fair guide to her strength and ability but there's a lot more to her than just the numbers.

When Lindop drove Exalted Time up the Morphettville straight after a brilliant front-running ride in the 2006 Group 1 Adelaide Cup, it rewarded the efforts of a young woman not brought up to achieve such a feat. This was someone who, it seemed, had no right to be a leading rider, let alone someone setting Adelaide alight and one of the great role models for young girls coming through the ranks. She grew up at Wangoom, just outside of Warrnambool, the third and youngest daughter of teachers Clive and Maggie in a non-racing family. But she loved horses and she was determined.

So Mum and Dad let her ride ponies from the age of ten, which led to trail riding along the local Hopkins River and eventually an apprenticeship with a local trainer.

'A man named John Lee really introduced me to horses and I would spend all my spare time riding horses with his grandsons,' she recalls. 'I rode all different sorts of ponies so I knew they all had to be treated differently. Different skills were required. From Shetland ponies to Clydesdales. Johnny introduced me to a local trainer Frank Byrne and I started working for him on the weekends from about the age of thirteen, and the twenty dollars I was paid to work at the stable allowed me to look after my pony, Annie. It was fantastic.

'Eventually Frank asked me to ride trackwork so I thought I'd give it a go. I'll always remember coming back in after going through a trot one, canter one situation. The horse was so strong that when I came back, my legs were like jelly and my arms were shaking. I thought this is totally different to riding a pony. I would catch the school bus from the stable and then, halfway through Year 9, I realised this was the career I wanted. There was some resistance from Mum in particular but I left school at the end of the year to become a jockey. If I had a fifteen-year-old daughter who wanted to leave school at the end of Year 9 to become a jockey, I'd be horrified as well.'

Lindop remembers learning plenty with Byrnes but, despite winning her first metropolitan race for the trainer at Moonee Valley, opportunities were limited and she transferred to leading district trainer Jack Barling in 1998. She got a lot of rides all over the state with the new stable but

Barling became terminally ill and she had to make a decision about her future as the stable closed down. Experience in the south-east of South Australia and on a couple of trips to Morphettville prompted her to move interstate — and to start one of the greatest South Australian riding careers.

'I still claimed three kilograms in the city and I didn't think I'd get a look at them in Melbourne,' she recalls. 'I spoke to chief steward at the time, Graham Loch, and he arranged for me to do three months with Byron Cozamanis. I came to Adelaide in July 1999 and finished my time in May 2000. Going to Cozy was brilliant because he put me on everything and I was leading rider in Port Lincoln and got plenty of provincial winners. All my rides when I came out of my time were pick-up rides on the minimum and I really didn't think I'd make a city jockey. I thought my career would be that of a country jockey.'

Lindop remembers 'a whole chain of events' led to her establishment as a serious senior rider in the early 2000s. Her work ethic and preparedness to travel might have had a bit to do with it too.

'I had won the Broken Hill Cup on Vanderclare in 2002 and the next day, I got a pick-up winner for David Hayes at Balaklava. The next minute, David Balfour called me and said his owners wanted me to ride a good mare of theirs called Agalia. Balf gave me a lot of opportunities and all of the sudden I was riding winners in the city, then I started to become a second rider for Leon [Macdonald] when Jason Holder couldn't ride those on the minimum.'

That chain of events took Lindop all the way to the 2001–02 country jockeys premiership but all the wins didn't amount to anywhere near as much as one win produced in the autumn of 2003. The winning ride on Debben in the South Australian St Leger was to have massive ramifications — the mare went on to run in that year's Melbourne Cup and Lindop retained the ride. She started a despised $201 outsider and finished nineteenth to the legendary Makybe Diva but it was just the opportunity the young rider needed.

'That changed my life,' Lindop says. 'Riding in that Melbourne Cup was a complete game changer. I was on TV everywhere, on panel shows, I was on Roy & HG's show, I met Paris Hilton. I was a superstar for a week.

'I think the feeling from other owners/trainers was that if Leon Macdonald thought she was good enough to ride in the Melbourne Cup, then she must be alright.'

The opportunities increased, and so did the winners. In one week, Lindop rode four winners at a meeting on three occasions and finished the season with 111 winners. It was a record at the time for a woman rider, surpassing Bev Buckingham's one hundred season wins.

'Although I was proud of the fact I was part of history, I found that the fame was a doubled-edged sword, though,' Lindop says. 'The media wanted to talk to me because I was supposedly the first girl to ride in a Melbourne Cup and then they were so disappointed to find out that I wasn't. Maree Lyndon and Linda Ballantyne had ridden in it already. Then I told them I was the first Australian woman and they thought, fine we'll go with that angle. They wanted a first girl story. Perhaps the real story was that, after two New Zealand jockeys rode in the Melbourne Cup in the eighties, it took fifteen years before another woman rode in the race.

'All through my career, I've had to say no I'm not the first girl to do this or that. All those girls in the eighties and nineties worked so hard but then there was a big gap between female riders coming through. After me, more girls came on the scene. The same year that I won my first metropolitan premiership here, Kathy O'Hara won the New South Wales apprentice title. Alana Samson was doing good things in Western Australia, Jodie Borett was leading rider in Tasmania. Suddenly girls were getting the opportunity and now it's standard practice.'

Lindop is well known for her strong, no-nonsense views on the gender debate. She has never wanted to be labelled a woman jockey or someone who has achieved plenty 'for a woman'.

'I got annoyed with the constant stream of gender questions,' she says. 'In one of my interviews before I rode Dolphin Jo in the 2007 Melbourne Cup, I was fairly scathing to a journalist in the parade. I regret the way I spoke to him because he was really quite a nice guy but I reacted to being asked how I felt about being a girl in the Melbourne Cup. I snapped at him that I'm not here because I'm a girl, I'm here because I've ridden the horse, I know the horse, I can make the weight, I have a good relationship with [trainers] Terry and Karina O'Sullivan and I think I can give the horse its best chance. I got pissed off with that media mentality before the big race.'

Lindop proved her confidence in Dolphin Jo when the five-year-old gelding ran a slashing fifth, beaten just over three lengths, to Efficient. She had given the $61 outsider, who had been unplaced at his previous two Group 2 starts, every chance and earned connections more than $160,000. She got another ride next year, this time with Cups King Bart Cummings and was on a live outside chance as she took $31 roughie Moatize to the barriers. She rode another faultless race on the Danehill Dancer four-year-old — in contrast to the three Aidan O'Brien runners who went out too fast and were beaten before the turn — but she had to settle for an another unplaced cheque.

'When the three O'Brien horses, who went out at a ridiculous pace, came back to the field at the top of the straight, I thought "holy shit, I can win the Melbourne Cup"' she says. 'Then Viewed went straight past us but we hung on well for sixth.'

Getting a Melbourne Cup ride, Lindop believes, is as much about reputation as it is gender. She points out that those jockeys who ride perfect races for no result get no credit but they are quickly criticised if they ride a poor one.

She may not have claimed racing's biggest prize in 2008 but she came close. Three days earlier, Lindop defied the odds when she guided Rebel Raider home a $101 winner of one of the world's great classics, the Group 1 Victoria Derby. It was a victory as much for the jockey's determination and racing knowledge as it was her riding ability.

'Rebel Raider bombed out in the Hill Smith Stakes [in Adelaide] and Leon said I didn't have to go to Geelong to ride him in the Derby Trial but I wanted to ride him because I knew he was going alright,' she says. 'He ran a place in the trial and I said let's try the blinkers in the Derby. If he'd won the Hill Smith and the Derby Trial, though, I'm not sure I'd have got the ride. I don't think it's because I'm a woman either, he'd have been considered a big chance instead of a 100/1 shot and they'd have looked for a top Melbourne rider.'

That's exactly what happened three years later, when Lindop lost the Caulfield Cup ride aboard talented mare Southern Speed. Again, she puts losing that ride down to the pursuit of a carnival jockey, with internationally-recognised Craig Williams getting the ride.

'I'm pretty sure the owners didn't think I was good enough, even though I'd won a Victoria Derby a couple of years earlier,' she says. 'It's frustrating but it's racing. I got beaten on Southern Speed in the Oaks in Adelaide in the autumn and that upset one of the owners in particular. It's their right to change riders and Craig won the race but I have no doubt I would have achieved the same result.

'You have to take the highs with the lows. I've had tremendous support from the word 'go'. When I was with Cozy, a few owners said let's try someone else, meaning a male apprentice, but he said "No, Clare rides everything". So I certainly can't say I had people up against me as a woman rider. Maybe there were people on the outside against me, but not with the people I was riding for.

'I saw some girls ride with what I'd call a chip on their shoulder, saying they wouldn't get a go because they were a girl. I know where they were coming from but I refused to accept it and just kept trying to improve myself.

'I looked up to some very strong female riders who really showed they could mix it with the men, riders like Therese Payne, Maree Payne and Christine Puls. I tried to look at what it might be that people perceived in a woman rider. I figured they thought girls weren't as strong as the male riders. If they think you're not as strong as a guy, get stronger than the guys. If they think you can't speak as well as the guys, learn to speak better. I thought it was all about improving myself and not giving them the excuse to take me off a horse or not give me the ride. Even now, I think it's a copout to say they're taking you off just because you're a female jockey. I think they usually just want a change of rider.

'An issue women riders have is that if we don't get enough chances at carnival times. I can understand an owner with possibly their one chance to win a Cox Plate or Melbourne Cup selecting a jockey who's won the race half-a-dozen times. That's why you need the support of someone to believe in you and for you to work hard to establish your relationship with that horse and the connections, and that applies to all jockeys, male or female.

'As an example, my biggest supporter, Leon Macdonald, will say, "Clare might not be the best jockey, but she's the best jockey for me" ... meaning he knows I will be trying to perform my absolute best at all times, which at the end of the day is all anyone can do. The problem isn't just those owners on that big occasion, it's the lack of opportunities women have had throughout the years to prove themselves.

'One of the issues to come out of Michelle's Melbourne Cup win, I think, is that the story appealed to the mainstream media and consequently became a 'men against women' saga but didn't seem to change the thinking in racing circles.'

Lindop has had to stick to South Australia to pick up her two other Group 1 wins — the 2009 South Australian Derby, also aboard Rebel Raider, and the 2011 Goodwood

Handicap on Lone Rock. The four Group 1s might be the highlights but the day-to-day, week-to-week attitude is what's brought Lindop the 2005–06, 2007–08 and 2014–15 Adelaide premierships.

'As a sixteen-year-old having my first ride, I was terrible,' Lindop recalls. 'But I was persistent and refused to give anyone an excuse to not book me for a ride. If I had an injury, I tried not to show it. If I wasn't well, I'd suck it up and work through it. I wasn't very good with the whip so I worked on it and became very good with the whip. Then when the whip rules changed, I made sure I changed for the better with them. I've always tried to make myself the best option. I'm proud of what I've achieved.'

# Racecaller

## VICTORIA SHAW

She is an accomplished racecaller who picks up a few greyhound races every Sunday afternoon as well as the occasional bush meeting. She is an astute commentator with the ability to host major functions around the world and domestic racing's increasing number of social events but her biggest achievements have come in Poland, the United States and the United Arab Emirates.

Victoria Shaw may be the perfect illustration of the modern woman's struggle in Australian racing.

She is forced to work a day job away from racing, these days as a temp in a legal office, still unable to find full-time industry employment in the busiest racing nation on earth. It sounds like a throwback to another age that there would be a question over whether a woman could call a race as well as a man, based solely on gender. But the numbers don't lie. No women currently call full TAB race meetings in Australia, even though one has been putting her name forward for almost twenty years. Shaw did call a complete Pioneer Park meeting in Alice Springs in 2008 but it didn't lead to more of the same.

Shaw is a strong, vocal woman who suspects she may have upset the male-dominated racing establishment by calling out the biases, bullying and sexual harassment to which she has been tediously subjected at various stages of her career.

'I had one situation where a prominent television sports director asked me to a business meeting at a hotel, then when I got there, sent a message for me to go to his room,' she recalls. 'I was a bit naive and went to the room and realised straight away that I shouldn't have. He was with another well-known but not necessarily well-respected identity, shoes off, drinks in hand, obviously looking for more than a business meeting.

'When you report this sort of stuff, you're considered the troublemaker for bringing it up. Who's going to make it up? It's about time some of these guys grew up and their employers took claims like this seriously.

'I have had opportunities but they are few and far between. I get a couple of opportunities a year and then I disappear again. They bring me out at Spring Carnival time to pretend I'm getting a fair go but nothing ever goes any further.

'Too often, I am brought in for hosting work at fashions on the field events. I really appreciate the work and often enjoy the days but there's more to racing than clothes and, after all, I am a racecaller. You would think that, even when I get these jobs, they would use me to call a race or two. That's the attitude I'm dealing with, that I'm a woman and my place is to host certain functions as long as they don't have a lot to do with the business of running a race.'

Shaw is not critical of all men in the industry, far from it. She is very clear about the support she has received from most male racecallers, the very people against whom she would be competing for work.

'I've been given a lot of support by these guys, they've been great,' she says. 'Greg Miles has been incredibly helpful and I've also had a lot of support from Rob Testa, who has gone out of his way to get me races to call at the greyhounds.

'I didn't grow up with greyhound racing but it's taught me so much. The speed of the race means, as Rob told me, you have to be able to edit in the run.

'I'd be nowhere without the support of people like John Russell, Rob Testa, Greg Miles, Steve Hawkins, Brian Markovic and Ray Benson, all men who are very good at what they do and have been very supportive. I just think it all comes back to the desk jockeys who think we're maybe going to upset someone at the TAB. Many of these guys are parents with daughters and they're sitting there wondering "what the heck is going on?"

'This isn't a 'woman against man' thing, I've received a lot of support from many very decent men who are horrified at the obstacles I've faced and continue to come up against.'

It's been a long haul for Shaw, who grew up in the Dandenongs and decided in her twenties she wanted to be a racecaller. Now in her mid-forties, she is still working for the opportunity to be able to do the job day-in, day-out. Not that she hasn't seized any opportunity that's come along and built a very impressive resume. She's called the HH Sheikha Fatima Bint Mubarak Ladies World Challenge, moderated the Women in Racing Conference in Poland and co-hosted the Arabian Racing Awards at Hollywood's Dolby Theatre weeks after the Oscars were held.

It's unfortunate, perhaps, that Shaw's best opportunities and memories have come overseas. Like the day she stood next to English Channel Four and ITV commentator Derek Thompson and Ladbrokes broadcaster Gary Capewell on the Tor Sluzeweic balcony in Warsaw, looking out over the art deco architecture to the 600 metre home straight and the vast course behind it.

'Calling in Poland was the greatest day of my career,' she recalls. 'Derek told me that day that we were standing at one of just four structures in all of Warsaw that Hitler did not destroy. It was extremely moving.

'I've got an Englishman either side of me, I've got a tote board in Cyrillic language and I'm an Australian calling women from all around the world for an Arabic network with a German crew.

'I will always remember it. Bouchra Marmoul, Morocco's first female jockey and a Muslim woman winning her first race. It was abroad, broadcast live on Yas Sports TV, the Arabic channel owned by HH Sheik Mansoor Bin Yazed Al Nahyan, the Crown Prince of Abu Dhabi. This young girl was coming up the home straight on a dapple grey called Wassilew. The female jockeys in this event were not allowed to use the whip, so Bouchra was all hands and heels and you could see her tiring close to home but doing everything she could to lift this horse over the line. The horse won by a short half head and, as she turned the horse around to come back to the enclosure after the race, she was in tears as she stood up in the irons.

'It brought tears to my eyes too. All the problems I've experienced at home, this occasion made me forget about all the nonsense and the bullshit in Australia. It just reminded me at the time, aren't we here to bring races to life?'

The problem for Shaw is that, as a girl who grew up watching races in Melbourne, she wants to call races in her home town or at least in her own country for a job. That is always brought back to her every time she returns from one of her overseas stints but then the jobs don't come.

'Anyone who comes through as the first to do something will always encounter resistance,' she says. 'It's sad and it's small minded but it's true. I've had a few networks asking if they could film me calling a race and I've always wondered why, the action's on the track.

'It's extremely Australian, unfortunately. We are looking like an international joke. When I went abroad for the first time with this Arabian tour, I was astounded by all the things that are not reported here. It was jaw dropping.

'Racing is the best societal barometer anywhere in the world. After more than a century, we still have resistance to women in racing yet the Sheikh Mansoor Bin Zayed Al Nahyan series has been going for seven years and it's creating social reform.

'We are sitting here assuming the absolute worst of some of these countries when women jockeys are getting opportunities in Morocco, Egypt, Bahrain, Oman, the UAE and Tunisia.'

Shaw insists she has been something of a victim of the 'don't rock the boat' mentality sometimes found within businesses with a strong sense of establishment. Like racing.

'I'm not saying I'm going to be the greatest caller in the world, all I've ever wanted was to start at the start,' she says. 'Some people in racing management positions have been negative and, to be honest, pretty limited. I've been told several times that the problem with having a woman racecaller is that punters might not accept it.

'It's ridiculous that too many people running racing without any imagination are worried that the typical punter might be offended by a woman racecaller. They actually believe that, and they don't want to upset anyone. What they don't understand, a part of the sheer bigotry of that thinking is that punters will still bet whether a man or a woman calls the race. What are they going to do? Stop betting. In Australia? Not likely. I can't imagine too many punters saying, "no I'm not betting on that good thing because that sheila's calling the race". It's just laughable.

'What Australian racing is kowtowing to is that same moronic individual featured in ads with the message "please don't bash your wife, it's not nice". To believe the average man in a TAB is a knuckle-dragging troglodyte just insults men in general.

'I've met many, many good men in racing. RV engaged James Fremantle, a real professional with impressive credentials, who recommended I was ready to call. Greg Miles made recommendations, among which I was ready to call the trials. Then nothing came of it. I have to ask, why engage these people if you're not going to act on their recommendations?

'I really believe they did that simply in case I cried foul and they got hauled in by the Equal Opportunity

Commission. It basically wasted twelve months of my life. Greg [Miles] has been a huge source of inspiration right throughout my adult life and, to drag him into this mess defies belief. I'm sure he has better things to do with his time.'

For all of the obstacles she has faced, Shaw remains passionate about the work she does and the full-time career she still strives to make of it. She remembers the first time a race call inspired her and the path it set her on all those years ago.

'When I was in my early twenties, I was in the car listening to a race call from Brian Markovic where a 100/1 shot won and it was just so remarkable the way he described every aspect of it,' she recalls. 'I felt, listening to the call, that I was there catching the excitement of the event, the shock within the crowd, all from this one race call. I had no money on the horse, no interest in the race but it transported me there. That's when I decided I wanted to be a racecaller.

'The audio of a race, without even having to see it, can excite you and capture your imagination. John Russell told me early on that I needed to get some practice to know what it feels like to call a live race so he set me up in the box next to him at the 1997 VRC Grand National and I called it into my tape recorder. I think I did a fair job. I got some very helpful feedback and advice, and I've gone on from there.'

Indeed she has. Shaw's work schedule reads like a travelogue or, more accurately perhaps, the log book of a seasonal worker. In 2016, she called at the Gold Coast in September, returned to Melbourne to call the Sandown Park dogs and even had a job calling on Melbourne Cup Day —

a five-race non-TAB card at Coffs Harbour. She's called at Morphettville and Caulfield, just not for local consumption. In Adelaide, she called for the Dubai international racing channel and the Melbourne job was for Yas TV live to Abu Dhabi.

With the Australian opportunities remaining limited and sporadic, Shaw has no choice other than to look abroad. She has plans to call at Abu Dhabi with colleague Terry Spargo, Morocco is on the horizon and she hopes to be given the opportunity to work at Jebel Ali and Meydan.

'I'm one piece in the puzzle of this incredible social reform being led out of the Middle-East and that's what keeps me going,' she says. 'There's been such change in a short space of time in some of these countries, while we still struggle to put women on horses and have trouble accepting them as racecallers or in management positions. Contrary to what we may believe here, I'm meeting people from many Muslim countries with much broader minds than what some people have in Australia.

'I enjoy the work I'm getting overseas but I've also been forced to take it because it's not available here. I got paid several weeks wages for an hour-and-a-half's work in the UAE the last time I was there. I have a mortgage to pay so I take the work where and when it comes.'

It's something of a blight on Australian racing that Shaw has to continue to travel overseas to find it.

## Syndicator

# DENISE MARTIN

Denise Martin wouldn't consider herself a matchmaker. She was an upmarket hotel executive with hands-on experience dealing with wedding parties and, at one point, she contemplated becoming a marriage celebrant — but never a matchmaker.

In an anomalous way, though, that's exactly what she's been doing for more than twenty years as the founder of Star Thoroughbreds, Australia's largest racehorse syndication company that's matched equine bluebloods with owners and brought people together from all over Australia and the world. Quite an achievement for a woman who grew up in Tasmania and started out in a teaching career — although it must be said she was always exposed to sport and, later, horse racing.

Born into a great sporting family on the Apple Isle, Denise's father Geoffrey 'Paddy' Martin was inducted into the Tasmanian Sporting Hall of Fame in 2015 for his achievements in football, cricket and running. An Australian Rules icon, he later turned his attention to training racehorses, giving a young Denise an introduction into the sport. Paddy Martin sold Adidas, Puma and Nike footwear before they became household names and that brought his daughter into contact with elite sportspeople like the legendary Ron Clark and champion footballer Peter Knights, both of whom became family friends and would visit when in Tasmania.

'Dad had always followed racing and he had friends in Victorian racing so in my teenage years, I followed racing more than most people knew and certainly more than was expected of a girl,' Denise Martin recalls. 'Then I left school, I got a teaching degree and taught in Tasmania for a few years before heading overseas for what turned out to be six years away. During that time, almost by accident and certainly not by design, I became involved in the luxury hotel business and that working holiday job became a twenty-two-year career.'

It was when Martin returned to Melbourne that she renewed her interest in racing — both socially and professionally. A mix of work responsibilities and sheer good fortune put her in touch with a woman destined to become one of the greats of world racing.

'Just over twenty years ago, I was in Melbourne and knew a lot of people in the racing business and I decided I wanted to start my own business as a challenge,' she says. 'I would look down from the top floor of the fifty-storey hotel on a Friday and Saturday and see weddings being held and I came up with the idea of becoming a marriage celebrant. But that presented problems. I was media and marketing director at the Regent in Melbourne, where they hosted a lot of weddings, and I found out that it would be a conflict of interest to keep working and run the business — and I needed to keep working in case the business fell over. Also, of course, the hotel industry was my career at the time and I couldn't afford to jeopardise it.

'Through my contacts with the VRC and friends in the racing industry in Melbourne, I thought there had to be a way of working in racing in some capacity. I thought: I didn't want to work for a stud because I was committing too much time to the hotel business, I don't want to work for a media outlet, I wanted to work for me. What could I do? I thought, well I could breed horses but then I'd have to buy a farm. I could train horses — no, too early in the morning for me. Then I thought I might investigate racehorse syndication. So I contacted a friend of mine in Melbourne and asked her if she knew a good accountant to help me to apply for my syndicators license in Victoria. She put me on to Spectrum Accounting in Carlton and my accountant there said, yes it could be done but he needed to know which trainer I'd be using. I'd never thought of that. So I contacted a couple of top trainers in Melbourne but they thought it was a bizarre notion that a successful hotel executive would want to be a racehorse syndicator and maybe I should stick to working in the hotel business.

'As luck would have it, Gai Waterhouse had just been granted her trainers' license and I asked her if she'd come and talk to me. I invited her and [husband] Rob [Waterhouse] to stay at the Regent when they came down for the 1993 Melbourne Cup and we had Dermot Weld and Michael Kinane on another floor of the hotel.'

It was the perfect scenario. Vintage Crop created history winning the Cup for Weld and Kinane, while Gai Waterhouse, in her first try at the great race, trained outsider Te Akau Nick to run a brave second after leading well into the straight. The hotel was full of happy people, Waterhouse was more enthusiastic than ever and Martin had the perfect opportunity to run a business idea by the woman who would go on to become a legend of Australian racing.

'I had breakfast with Gai the next morning and told her I was applying for a syndicator's license, would she consider working with me?', Martin recalls. 'She said, "I'd love to". It took three months for the license to be approved and I packed up everything and moved to Sydney. It was a major change for me but I threw myself into it and I was off on a new leg of my life. I remember staying at the Regent as a guest before leaving and when I was all packed for Sydney, on the same day the Rolling Stones arrived for a tour, the concierge said he wasn't sure who had the most luggage.'

That was early 1994. Martin took up residence at Tulloch Lodge, where she stayed for twenty years and built her idea for racehorse syndication into the massive Star Thoroughbreds operation that has become known and respected around the globe. She finally left the iconic Randwick stable in 2013 — on good terms with her dear friend Gai — when she knew it was time for a new chapter and challenge in her life. Martin left the horses already at Tulloch Lodge with Waterhouse and took Star Thoroughbreds to the Rosehill stables of Chris Waller. It was a bold move but, in the Denise Martin way, turned out to be yet another successful decision.

'I needed a change and I identified Chris as a remarkable

trainer,' she says. 'Gai was surprised but she understood my need for a change and it's worked very well. I left sixty-five horses at Tulloch Lodge and encouraged the owners to stay with Gai and I've bought about twenty-five horses a year since leaving there for Chris to train. Currently, I have about sixty horses on Chris' books.'

Martin certainly joined the Waller stable at an opportune time, with the New Zealander racing to the top of the Sydney training ranks and about to transform Winx from outstanding filly to world champion mare. The times ahead are exciting but there's never been a period in the Star Thoroughbreds era when things have been any less than exhilarating. The years from 2010 to 2013 were nothing short of breathtaking, with a string of Group 1 victories in Melbourne and Sydney and the exceptional Sebring delivering a Golden Slipper.

'Sebring won the Slipper and has become an unbelievably successful stallion, so I have no doubt he's the best horse we've had, but there have been many very good horses and real money-spinners,' she says. 'Probably my favourite, the one that holds a special place in my heart, is Theseo. He won five Group 1s and almost three-and-a-half million dollars and he was a genuine warhorse who always gave his best.'

The Sebring story is the stuff that gets people excited about syndication: adding the G1 AJC Sires' Produce to the Slipper win before being sold to Widden Stud in the Hunter Valley for $28 million. While not everyone can be in a syndicate that shares that level of success and reward, Martin continues to promote thoroughbred syndication as not just a potential moneymaking opportunity but a great way to get involved in the industry and enjoy the social benefits that come with it at an affordable price. She says she's proud that her work has brought more women to the races and given some a social life they may otherwise have missed.

'I worked on the basis that I wanted to try and offer a style of racing that hadn't been fully explored at that time,' she says. 'It was an opportunity to meet likeminded people, get them together at the racetrack and make friends or acquaintances that way. It allowed people to meet at the track and develop friendships that flourished away from the races.

'We have owners who have been to Royal Ascot and to the Hong Kong International week as a group. Without the horses, they wouldn't have had that opportunity. We have a lot of people, male and female, who are on their own and they're happy to come along and meet other people.

'When I established the Star Thoroughbreds, I made up my mind that I would stay involved in the horses and the people. We open the stables for members to come and see their horses every second Sunday of the month; we take them to the Hunter Valley horse studs and we have great social days out. I've found women are every bit as interested in thoroughbred racing as men. It's amazing the number of people who have made close personal friendships out of being in a syndicate and I'm proud that a lot of these are women who would have been lost to racing without that involvement.'

Photographer

# SHARON LEE CHAPMAN

If Clare Lindop and Michelle Payne have resisted being known as the best female jockeys in Australia, it's fair to assume Sharon Lee Chapman wouldn't appreciate being a contender for best female photographer title either.

Her images are as much art as they are racing photography, the pictures jumping off magazine pages and computer screens, and gender has nothing to do with it.

When Gai Waterhouse cut a lonely figure during early morning trackwork at Newmarket, Chapman was there capturing the great trainer through the mist.

When Waterhouse collected her first Melbourne Cup with Fiorente and when Chris Waller accepted the Cox Plate for his superstar Winx, Chapman was there snapping the news photos as well as the character shots.

When an anonymous horse trod water at Altona Beach and when syndicate members, dressed in their finery, enjoyed their fifteen minutes of glorious fame after any one of a hundred race wins, she was there also to capture the stark contrasts of the Australian racing landscape.

Chapman acknowledges she was fortunate to capture the image that announced her arrival as a serious racing photographer but she has certainly built on that luck with hard work and rare expertise.

It was May 2011 and she had taken the day off work to venture down to Warrnambool for the Grand Annual Steeplechase. She had the lens tracking the leaders, who were racing wide apart, for the type of artistic shot that has become her signature. She couldn't have expected what was to come next. When Banna Strand threw the rider and continued running before veering off course and leaping a two-metre-plus barrier into a crowd of up to one hundred people, she was the only snapper to capture the freak incident. Seven people were injured — fortunately none too seriously — and the photo was on the front page of the *Herald Sun* the next day, then went around the world to appear in the *New York Times* and *Washington Post*. The photo went on to garner a major award, not simply in the sports category but the coveted Quill Award for Victorian News Photo of the Year.

'Rather than stay at the jump like everyone else was, I just tracked the two horses to get a mood shot with the huge crowd behind them,' Sharon recalls. 'If you stay on the jumps, you're not getting the whole atmosphere of the event. I got lucky because something unexpected happened but I wouldn't have got the shot if I was doing what all the men were doing.'

Not bad for someone who didn't even have a media pass and got a day pass from friend George Vella of TVN. That day changed everything for Chapman, who was doing weddings while working in paralegal conveyancing on a contract basis with Slater and Gordon after working for another law firm, Wisewould Mahony, and travelling to the United States every Australian winter for four years to shoot summer camp action in Pennsylvania.

'Slater and Gordon wanted to me renew my contract when I came back from the US but the Banna Strand photo got me to make a tough decision about my photographic career,' she recalls. 'I had been given a break when I picked up work taking trackwork and stable photos with the John Salanitri stable but I was still well and truly on the fringe as a racing photographer. I thought "I'm just going to throw this open to the universe and see what happens."'

It wasn't an easy assignment Chapman set for herself but somehow she made the constraints of coming into the fold as a relative outsider work for her. It's almost as though she knew that, in order to make it as a racing photographer, she had to take a better or at least more original photo than the next person. And so she did.

'Some of the best photos I've taken have been when I've not been able to get the prime position for the news pic or the return to scale,' she says. 'What that means, though, is that I'm going to get something different to everyone else. As a freelancer, you have to use your imagination because you don't have the number one position and it doesn't always pay off when a horse goes a different direction or the clerk's horse is in the way. What's the point of me getting the shot that forty other people can get? My value is to go for the risky shot.'

Like many women in the Australian workplace,

Chapman has experienced a degree of outdated and sometime boorish behaviour that's made her job more difficult than it needed to be. She is quick to point out that it's a declining trend, even if racing has been a little slow on the uptake at times.

'I can't say I've experienced any outright sexism,' she says. 'I did get a lot of bullying from a couple of male photographers but that wasn't typical of the guys in the media room. One of these men was bullying men as well and the other one threatened to kill me and I had to get a restraining order. He breached the restraining order five times and ended up getting arrested, and of course he lost his racing credentials. I was a single female getting recognition for my work and that, combined with my small stature, made me an easy target I suppose.'

Chapman is perhaps more forgiving about what she went through than many others would be, preferring to move on and take the next great photo: 'You face some interesting challenges and you just have to believe that people like this get rubbed out of the industry.'

Despite the remarkable quality of Chapman's images, her quest for still greater excellence took her to Colorado in 2015 for a photographic workshop to improve every aspect of her work.

'If you thought you were getting good or if you needed a reality check, that workshop soon put things into perspective,' she recalls. 'I learned so much there. But I also met a woman there, a picture editor for *Sports Illustrated*, who liked my work and invited me to go to New York. I was heading to New York anyway so the timing was perfect and, of course, I'd have never given up the opportunity. That had a ripple effect and opened a lot of doors.'

Chapman pitched the idea of a Birdsville races shoot to *Sports Illustrated* and quickly found her images published as the company's coveted *Viewfinder Weekly* online spread. Her work is featured prominently and regularly in the upmarket Swedish racing magazine *Gallop* and her images adorn racing journals, newspapers and industry websites right around Australia.

Since going full-time, she has covered Royal Ascot, the Cheltenham Festival, the Dubai World Cup, Hong Kong International Day, the Singapore Cup, Saratoga and famously photographed Triple Crown winner American Pharoah winning the Haskell Invitational at Monmouth Park. For all of her overseas travels, a photo of the great Winx striking a stately pose in knee-deep water at Altona beach encapsulates everything that makes Sharon Lee Chapman a photo artist.

'It was the Sunday before the Cox Plate and I got up at 3.30am leaving my house in Mornington to drive to Altona on the off-chance Winx would be there,' she recalls. 'As the other photographers lined the beach, I knew the money shot was going to be Winx in the water with the city skyline behind her. In order to get the shot, I ventured out further than anyone, with the water up to my waist, standing on tiptoes to keep my cameras out of the water. As soon as she stopped there for a moment, I knew it had been worth the risk.

'The fact she went on to win the race a second time and stamp herself a great champion justifies the decision to shoot the pic that way because now it isn't just another photo of a horse working. It captured a moment in time.'

Sharon Lee Chapman continues to capture moments in time every time she sets foot on a racetrack, a training facility, a beach where horses go through their paces or into the stalls of the biggest and smallest stables. She's clearly a skilled practitioner but it's her eye for the unexpected and her passion for the sport and industry that sets her apart and makes her an invaluable asset to racing. It shows in the joy of winning owners, the ripple of muscle on our finest thoroughbreds, the relief of a trainer whose champion has won again and the packed and empty tracks across the country. In other words, every aspect of Australian racing.

Breeder

# CATHY HAINS

From the moment Cathy Hains bought into the world of thoroughbred breeding in the late eighties, she's made commercial viability and strong business principles a cornerstone of her operation. She could have cruised on the deeds of her business-mogul father and one of the greatest racehorses the world has ever seen but that wasn't going to take her or the business forward.

Hains' father, David, had succeeded in most aspects of the business world and it was no different when, on the advice of good friend and golfing legend Norman Von Nida, he bought a mare called Ada Hunter. In what Cathy Hains describes as a mix of 'luck and good judgement', the mare won a few races before being mated with brilliant sprinter Bletchingly to produce no less than the immortal Kingston Town.

It was enough to get young Cathy interested in racing but not enough to encourage her to leave her day job in sales at Channel 9. She resisted her father's call for her to join the flourishing Kingston Park Stud until the business model was right for her to make the move.

'Whilst Dad had been keen for me to join, I felt more commercially inclined so waited until he was interested in selling some of the yearlings he bred,' she recalls. 'I joined the Kingston Park operation in the late 1980s.'

Hains recalls learning plenty about the breeding industry in her early years. David Hains was using groundbreaking methods by the early nineties and it was a great learning curve for a young woman with the commercial knowhow to make the most of it.

'Kingston Park had established an overseas breeding operation where Australian mares were sent to USA stallions and bred to Southern Hemisphere time,' she says. 'This was quite a unique concept at the time and a credit to my father's ability to think ahead of his peers at the time. The offspring born of Australian mares and champion USA horses travelled back to Australia after weaning and we sold the colts for a while.

'The early offerings brought a lot of interest at sale and I think we held the Australian record for the highest price colt sold for around ten years throughout the eighties and nineties. That colt was by Biscay and although he caused great excitement in the sale ring he was no superstar on track. Ironically, his less auspicious younger sister Riva Diva was retained and raced by Kingston Park and went on to win the early two-year-old races before taking out the [Group 1] Blue Diamond.'

Hains acknowledges she may never have got into the breeding industry if not for her father's friendship with Von Nida, who was not only his golf mentor but his early adviser on all aspects of racing.

'Norman was not only a world-class player but also a thoroughbred pedigree buff and his genuine interest, deep knowledge and great connections were responsible for the Hains family's entry into the world of racing,' she recalls.

'By luck or good judgement or probably a fair dose of both, the initial couple of modestly acquired horses won enough to pique my parents' interest and shortly afterwards my father and Norman decided to use his significant social resources to travel further afield to purchase some mares. Ada Hunter and Ursula Lauderdale were purchased from the world-renowned Dormella Stud in the seventies. Those fine mares were the dams of Kingston Town and Lowan Star and the rest is pretty much history.'

Lowan Star was an outstanding two-year-old filly who went on to win the AJC and Queensland Oaks; Kingston Town won three Cox Plates in his fourteen Group 1 wins, and was arguably the best horse in the world at the time. The performances of the likes of Kingston Town, in particular, whetted the appetite but Hains always had a desire to take things further in her own right.

'I bought Burnewang North from family interests in 2006 and we started a commercial breeding operation with a few modest mares we bought from Kingston Park, who were winding down a stallion station that had been based there for a few years,' Hains explains. 'The Farm is 2400 acres (971 hectares) of outstanding flat dry Northern Victorian cropping country just south of Echuca. It is great growing country and the temperate conditions are ideal for stock. We run around forty-five broodmares, some livestock and we grow winter and summer hay crops.'

Burnewang North Stud continues to have remarkable success in the sales ring, with a ninety-seven percent clearance rate of every yearling offered. More importantly for owners looking to get a return on their money, the stud has produced upwards of eighty individual winners in six countries. The record is credit to a young team Hains has put together and she is quick to point out that gender is never a consideration when she employs any woman — or man — on the team.

'I would hesitate to single out our staff by virtue of gender as they have been selected for numerous attributes and gender is not relevant,' she says. 'We do have outstanding woman on staff at Burnewang North — led by Emma Todd — and we are very proud of our young team's enthusiasm and dedication.

'Many of the breeding operations are run by capable and respected women — including luminaries such as Strawberry Hill, Makybe and Gilgai just to mention a few. I'm quite certain all these people maintain their standing in the business by virtue of their capabilities and accomplishments.'

While Hains doesn't give women or men any concessions when it comes to staffing — they simply have to be very good at what they do — she is pleased to note the value women are bringing into the breeding and racing industries. For a woman who believes everyone has to prove themselves, she is particularly proud of those women who have done just that.

'Outstanding women are becoming a lot more prevalent on the frontline of the modern breeding and racing operations,' she says. 'Women continue to make inroads in many areas of racing. On the ground, they are led by industry giants like Gai [Waterhouse], whose prominence and passion and resilience have inspired many and helped put our industry on the international stage.

'Others who spring to mind range from syndicator Denise Martin who I believe revolutionised syndication, before it became popularised, with her people skills, integrity and professionalism. Jenny McAlpine is another much-loved unsung hero (in her long career covering just about all aspects of breeding, racing and sales here and overseas) she has not only shone but she has quietly and selflessly connected more people in our industry to each other than just about anyone else I can think of.

'I also have a great deal of respect for women such as Caroline Searcy, Tara Madgwick and Francesca Cumani, who are polished and experienced commentators who keep us in the loop and who are not scared to have an opinion in the face of the dominating male pressure.

'I know I'm not alone here but I was delighted when champion jockey Michelle Payne not only showed her male counterparts how to achieve every jockey's dream, but was brave enough to call it as she saw it — bravo!

'Finally, I applaud and am grateful to strong corporate leaders such as Amanda Elliot and Katie Page, both of whose input at the business end of this complicated and competitive industry is inestimable.'

Hains firmly believes the racing industry needs to wake up and recognise the value of employing capable women in a range of roles — from the racetrack to the boardroom and all areas in between. She's not suggesting giving women any advantage over men. On the contrary, she just wants to see a level playing field.

'I believe women have to outperform the men considerably to gain credibility in this business,' she says. 'It continues to be a male-dominated sport that is not unlike many areas of big business which can be accused at times of paying lip service and little else in the equality stakes. Strong, determined and capable woman can overcome the challenges, and we see more of this happening every time we look around the track or the farm or the race club or the sale ring.

'But I can't help thinking that some of the men who proliferate those areas without opposition, and have done so since the beginning of our great sports and industry, have significantly less qualifications on many levels than many of their female counterparts who have had to work a lot harder to be counted.'

Judge

# NATASHIA RADFORD

Her father was a Californian surfie and her mother was born in New Guinea and raised in Singapore. Somehow, against odds that wouldn't appear on too many betting boards, Natashia Radford is building a career as the official judge at race meetings all over Victoria.

Born and raised in Brisbane, Radford may not have had the standard racing pedigree but, with a little help from a father who has always known how to read a formguide, created her own racing credentials. After leaving school, she moved to Sydney and worked as a stablehand for no less than Bart Cummings and if that's not good for a resume, nothing is.

Radford then moved to Canberra, where the encouragement of a male colleague while she picked up part-time weekend work led her to a career neither she, nor apparently the industry, ever imagined. What resulted was that, in the second decade of the twenty-first century, Australian racing employed its first female judge.

'Getting into judging was simply a matter of fate,' Radford

recalls. 'The chief judge at the time for Thoroughbred Park stood down and there was an opening for a trainee judge. I was working as a casual pool supervisor there every second Sunday and was approached by former jockey and Occ Health and Safety officer Garry Buchanan about the opportunity. I jumped at it. I passed my accreditation about eighteen months later and eventually moved to Victoria where I initially started judging harness races before an opening became available for a judge at Racing Victoria.'

Radford loves the work she is doing, travelling to racecourses around regional and rural Victoria, but makes no secret of her desire to go further.

'I have my sights on the Cup,' she says. 'With the increased number of races I am able to judge here in Victoria, compared to the amount with Racing New South Wales, my judging experience and skill has improved one hundred percent. I'm fortunate to be mentored by the best judge in the business. I am constantly learning tips from him, such as splitting tight margins or capturing sixteen horses crossing the finishing line within a split second of each other.

'As a bit of an adrenalin junky, the best part of the job is the satisfaction of splitting a tight finish. I get to see some of the best horses and jockeys race right in front of my eyes, seeing country Victoria and meeting lots of lovely people within the industry. The worst part is my love–hate relationship with a tight finish. I guess there really is no worst part of the job. I'm pretty excited to go judge at any racetrack I have not been to before.'

While it's taken decades longer than most areas of racing, Radford says she has had nothing but encouragement from the moment she set out on her historic course. The public reaction, she adds, has been overwhelmingly positive.

'I have not once felt held back or experienced a lack of opportunity as a woman within the racing industry,' she says. 'Maybe that is a good indication that things are changing. Racing Victoria, and more recently the VRC, have provided me with endless opportunities and they've given me the "sure you can do that" response whenever I've put my hand up for anything new. Yes, I am the first woman judge and I've attracted a few raised eyebrows whenever I turn up to a racecourse for the first time, but that blows over fairly quickly and people have been accepting and encouraging to me.'

The encouragement started from a young age, with father Marcus letting her look over his shoulder while he did the form. That, combined with a love and knowledge of horses, planted the seed for an unlikely racing career.

'My father is a keen punter so I learned to read the formguide from a young age,' she recalls. 'I also attended the local races while fairly young and my grandparents had a few syndicates but horse racing was a bit of a distraction and not the main topic of discussion at the dinner table.

'Every new racing experience has been an adventure. The first time I was introduced to jumps racing in my job, it just overwhelmed me. The power of the gallop, the sound of the horse as it brushes over the hurdle, the stretch of the horse's front legs over the jump. I was hooked. The Great Western Steeplechase, which is the oldest jumps race in Australia, was the first jumps race that I judged and it was remarkable.'

There's hardly an influx of women into traditional male roles but Radford expects it will change in the coming years. She's a career racing person and wants to reach the pinnacle of her field but she has no intention of moving into other areas of the industry. She is happy to stay in the judge's box and strive for excellence in the most important of racing roles.

'As long as my eyes are good and the brain is sharp,' she says, 'I hope to be doing this for a very long time.'

Promoter

# JENNIFER BARTELS

Jennifer Bartels wears many hats. Figuratively and literally. It's no coincidence that in one of her roles as a racing tour operator, she makes sure tourists get to stop in on a leading royal milliner in between visiting great racecourses.

When she's not showing racing first timers and experienced punters the world's great racing establishments, she is a member of the Queensland Horse Council, sits on the board of the Queensland Racehorse Owners Association, throws her support behind Griffith University's research into equine diseases and runs a list of social and fundraising events with the Women in Racing group on the Gold Coast.

Bartels insists on the need for good governance where owners are involved, believing ownership is a serious business, often emotional and at times costly, however exciting and exhilarating to be part of this scene.

'It is imperative to have female representation on Committees such as QROA, mostly to represent a minority in this industry which is seen to be male-dominated,' she says. 'Although I am neutral in this area, many ladies view the racing scene with hesitation. Fortunately, I have found great respect where women are participating.'

Bartels conducts tours every year to major race meetings and stallion tours of stud farms around the world. She says running such events brings new people, not just women, into the industry.

'It allows people to travel comfortably alone with people of a similar interest,' she says. 'It introduces those who may be interested in buying a thoroughbred to the best racing has to offer and lets them experience the industry first hand. It's not often a racegoer gets the opportunity to be introduced to trainers, owners and breeders from around the world and there are a lot of other social aspects to it as well — for instance, a visit to leading London milliners is a rare experience for many first timers.'

Bartels had one of her best experiences — and there have been many — when she met with great French trainer Criquette Head-Maarek in 2015 en route to Royal Ascot to watch Australian sprinter Brazen Beau race for the Ontrack Syndicate. It was in her role as the manager of Women in Racing that she detoured to magnificent Chantilly in Northern France to meet with the trainer of the legendary dual Arc De Triomphe winner Treve.

'Each year Women in Racing recognises one special female who has given outstanding performances in racing,' she explains. 'Criquette Head-Maarek was a particularly special recipient who stood out from the crowd. Highly respected and a brilliant lady trainer on the European scene, and with her success in getting Treve to the post for the second Arc win, we made her our decision based on her dedication and success in Europe.

'I travelled to Chantilly to present the award and spent three hours at training with Criquette. I then attended Royal Ascot for the Golden Jubilee Stakes where Brazen Beau, syndicated by Ontrack Thoroughbreds, ran a gallant second. He had been sold to Sheikh Mohammad for $10 million, however ran in the gold silks of Ontrack that day. It was a thrilling, exhilarating day.'

While not every event can be as breathtaking as a few hours at Chantilly with a world's best backdrop of the breathtaking 300-year-old Grandes Écuries (Great Stables), Bartels runs events throughout the year directed at improving the status of women within the industry. All guest speakers are expected to address a racing theme — with training, riding, fashion and ownership just a small sample of the diverse range of subjects. Over the past twelve years, the group has run in excess of 150 functions, raising substantial funds for Griffith University Equine Influenza Research.

'Griffith University is our selected racing welfare recipient,' she says. 'Their work is remarkable and necessary for the health of the industry. The Institute for Glycomics at Griffith University on the Gold Coast is an international leader in anti-microbial drug and vaccine development. We support the Institute and we're proud to provide funds for research into viral diseases that affect horses. Viruses such as equine influenza (EI) have had a significant impact on the racing industry in Australia and around the world and with recent outbreaks of Hendra virus much research is required to better understand their modus operandi.

'The Institute for Glycomics is cracking the code of these important viruses in the hope that new drugs may result. We are delighted to be supporting these outstanding scientists, under the guidance of Professor Mark von Itzstein, and look forward to the contribution their science will make to the horse industry.'

It's not all business and serious issues for Women in Racing, though, with the main theme to provide the sort of event that will excite new people and reward those already involved in the industry. Bartels says the many functions are the perfect way to meet new friends in racing and develop a new interest or take the next step and become more involved in the industry.

'Without hesitation, we have reached thousands of ladies over the years who have since purchased thoroughbreds, been involved in a syndicate, introduced them to the breeding side as well as the pleasure of a good day out at the track,' she says. 'The club has the nickname of Women E-m-b-racing and I think that's apt. It's a very enjoyable way to meet new friends, or to come along with old friends and just embrace all that racing has to offer.'

While Bartels welcomes just about any way to promote the cause of women in the racing industry, she stops short of using barely-dressed young women to promote events. She loves her Gold Coast racing but was not happy when the Gold Coast Turf Club allowed the running of the Bikini Girls Sprint on a day promoting Arabian horseracing.

'Any publicity is good publicity but I feel ladies jumping out of the barriers is akin to someone jumping out of a birthday cake,' she says. 'It's not even the bikinis or the semi-naked girls that is the main issue here, it's that they are being used to run like some sort of prop for our amusement. I think the context in which they are used is a bit demeaning and it's certainly not something racing should want to promote. I think we've come further than that.'

Bartels prefers to elevate the position of women in racing beyond light entertainment for men or groups. She wants to see them empowered and encouraged to get involved at all levels of racing. Fashion can feature, even provocative fashion, but she would like to see the day where the young women who raced down the track to the cheers of a boisterous crowd are given better opportunities to strut their stuff.

The list of key speakers at WIR functions has not been restricted to women. Far from it. Racing legends, current day greats and those actively involved in the promotion of racing have been equally represented by both genders — with Gai Waterhouse, John Letts, Mel Schumacher, Peter Moody, Sheila Laxon, Larry Olsen, Amanda Elliott, Matt Cumani, Bernadette Cooper, Jo McKinnon and Joe McGrath among the more recent guest speakers.

The list of award winners is diverse. It includes breeder Del Fitton, OAM, Brisbane Racing Club's Clerk of the Course Sarah Mannion, retired jockeys Bernadette Cooper, Pam O'Neill and Priscilla Schmidt and Magic Millions marketing manager Val Hayward along with Head-Maarek and 2017 recipient Gay Kelleway, the first woman jockey to win at Royal Ascot.

'During 2016 we further expanded our network including many new and valuable people through our events,' Bartels says. 'Of particular note was our guest speaker for the 2016 Magic on the Coast luncheon, Max Whitby. He's a breeder, syndicator, punter, racehorse owner and philanthropist and he's become a strong and enthusiastic supporter of WIR. Male or female, we need enterprising people of his calibre to come on board.'

Money and awareness raised from WIR luncheons and supporters have assisted a wide range of people and causes. It's helped apprentice jockeys get riding gear they could otherwise not have afforded and assisted those affected by injury or loss, including the family of Paula Shae Lane who lost her life in a trackwork accident at Roma's Bassett Park in 2005. It has promoted women already in the racing industry and been keen to help others get their start. And it has continued to promote recognition of the Griffith University research and provide financial support.

The group's media coverage, including the Magic Millions Official Luncheon and the annual pre-Melbourne-Cup tour, goes from strength to strength. They are all a source of pride for Bartels.

'Since we established WIR as a groundbreaking club totally new to the racing scene in Australia, I have noticed a quiet movement within the ranks of females in relation to the popular inclusion of female jockeys, trainers, owners and associations connected to racing,' she says.

'The number of female jockeys has certainly found favour with the public as they see it as a way of diversification and some as a novelty; the latter being a little inquisitive as to the results of riders. These ladies have met their goals by proving they are equally as good as most of the male jockeys.

'Determination is a key requisite for success as well as resistance to the male domination. Statistically, male jockeys have a big edge over female jockeys but that's largely because of the greater opportunities. Women jockeys are making headway, however. Similarly, women trainers are a little more accepted as their results improve with greater numbers.

'Discrimination is a word I am not comfortable with but it has been experienced by females anywhere on the track, especially in the jockeys' rooms. But some race clubs have recently made provisions for them and hopefully this will continue with other clubs around Australia. Unisex jockey rooms are simply not on my agenda.

'The general media industry is endeavouring to break this impasse and are featuring women commentators, tipsters and hosts, more so than ten years ago. This has been a resounding success for racing channels and has been embraced well by the listening audiences.

'Whether it's jockeys, trainers, breeders, bookmaker assistants, owners and media personalities, the industry has definitely improved and changed the scene for female participants.

'The future in racing for females has definitely changed and acceptance is growing in a way that suggests gender will be ignored in favour of talent. I'd like to think we've played a part in that.'

Trainer

# ALANA WILLIAMS

You hear the racing stories of kids growing up on a farm, riding before they can walk, giving school away to take up an apprenticeship, daughter or son of a great jockey or trainer. Alana Williams isn't one of them.

Williams had just one thing in common with most kids who wanted to become a jockey: she loved horses from a very early age. Everything else, including the racing industry, was foreign to her. She came from a working-class Perth family with no racing connections and her parents insisted she finish high school if she wanted to embark on a riding career.

That the young Alana Samson grew up to become an outstanding jockey, and then half of Perth's leading training combination with husband Grant Williams, is a story of hard work and determination as well as a rare ability waiting to be developed. In the eleven years between starting out as a tiny forty-one-kilogram apprentice in 1998 and riding her last race pregnant in 2009, Williams won 435 races and twenty-five at Group or Listed level.

'As little girls often do, I loved horses and ponies but I had virtually no idea the racing industry even existed,' she recalls. 'I came from a working-class family and it was an expensive hobby that I'd one day come to love. I got a job as a checkout chick in a supermarket at [age] sixteen, and earned enough to have the odd lesson, then I leased a horse and competed at pony club — and it went from there.

'A school teacher of mine, Steve Triscari, trained a couple gallopers. He used to do plenty work at the beach, so my first job with thoroughbreds was wading and swimming them at the beach and then exercising them at Steve's Baldivis property.

'I met another trainer, Darryl Cooper, who helped me get my trackwork license. He got me started on the track and learning my times to ride pace work. When I got enough confidence, I got a freelance license and started riding for other local trainers.'

All that came before Williams even started her apprenticeship. In fact, she hadn't even thought of race riding and only considered it when someone said that, at around thirty-nine kilograms, she should consider becoming a jockey. Inquiries about an apprenticeship led her to trainer David Harrison's Secret Harbour stables — but any racing work had to fit in with the education her parents insisted upon.

'My dad would drop me out there and wait for me to work between 5am and 8am every day, then it was a quick trip home for a shower then off to school,' she says. 'Mum and Dad said I could ride only if I finished Year 12 because the success rate for female jockeys in WA was almost nonexistent. So it was off to school, then I would go ride my own horse after school, followed up by dinner and homework, bed, and then do it all again the next morning.

'I signed up for my apprenticeship at seventeen on completion of high school and then, after completing the ten-week course at Muresk Ag. College, began trials almost immediately and started race riding in October 1998.

'My biggest hurdle was gaining the respect of the male jockeys. I didn't get much support within the ranks and I had to quickly develop a very thick skin or I wouldn't have lasted. Jockeys Paul King and Peter Knuckey helped me out a bit. Later on, I would watch Paul Harvey very closely, trying to pick up how he was so clever in races and what he did to make him better than the rest.'

Perhaps one of Williams' great assets is that she was always prepared to learn and has never forgotten those who have helped her along the way. Even today, as she and Grant head Perth training premierships, she remembers the support David Harrison and wife Jennie gave her in her developing years.

'Mr Harrison was sensational and very supportive,' she says. 'He and Jennie gave me a great opportunity and, even today, I regard them as mentors to Grant and me. They are happy for our success, and always the first to offer help. There were other good apprentices riding, and it was tough to get a go, so I was lucky to have bosses who had plenty [of] faith in me.

'I was lucky enough to get on some nice horses and had a couple of really good carnivals. I got to compete and win in Adelaide on Stormy Nova, who was my all-time favourite racehorse. We won the Sky Blue Stakes at Cheltenham and got beat a lip in the Yallambee Classic. And I got to ride outstanding horses like Fair Alert to win a Winterbottom Stakes and Asian Beau Stakes.

'One of the great things about my riding career was getting to meet some wonderful female jockeys who have been an inspiration. When I was in Melbourne on a three-month stint for Brian Mayfield-Smith, I met my idol Maree Payne and Sally Wynn. Later I met and became close friends with Clare Lindop and Bernadette Cooper.'

Williams met Cooper while they were riding in Manila. She also rode in Mauritius and twice in Malaysia, where she won a Magic Millions race and a couple of other features. Another friendship borne from racing has led to one of Perth's best trainer–rider partnerships — best friend Jessica Valas is the partner of champion jockey William Pike, who has since gone on to become the stable rider.

The evolution of Alana Samson, the top jockey to Alana Williams, the top trainer was always going to occur but it may have been sped up by a chance meeting with the man she would one day marry. As a twenty-something jockey, she met Grant Williams through trainer Lindsey Smith and it changed the course of her life. Alana and Grant, who was a prominent harness trainer, started dating and were soon married but they were some years away from making their training partnership official. While that was still evolving though, Williams was riding and pre-training up to eighteen horses for Smith.

'I took out a harness trainer's license and trained from

my ten-acre property in Karnup,' she recalls. 'I mucked around with a couple of Grant's hand-me-downs and did quite well, winning a handful of metro races with The Midnight Rocket. I even got him to the Group 1 Fremantle Cup. I learned how to drive pacers in harness, all while I was riding and pre-training.

'I was gradually getting out of the race riding, though, and only riding for the old boss and a few friends. Pre-training for Lindsey was important because he gave me lots of feedback to get better at it. Eventually Grant moved his team to my property so the pre-trainers went. Grant trained a couple gallopers as well and I rode them in races and we had a few winners. At this stage, I was winding right down with race riding, and Grant and I planned on starting a family. I was twenty-nine and although things were still going well I knew it was time. I had my last ride on Derby Day in 2009 and, at that stage, I was five weeks pregnant.'

The biggest change came when leviathan owner Bob Peters called with the offer to train four of his horses. Grant was still a solo trainer at that point but the offer gave them the confidence to consider a partnership. From the original four, he trained exceptional mare Delicacy to a Perth Cup, and the couple now have about forty of Peters' horses.

'It's been a whirlwind ride since having the Peters' family horses,' she recalls. 'I am thankful that someone like Mr Peters gave us the chance to train for him and has allowed us to make mistakes and learn along the way. We know we're lucky to have those horses, although it's coupled with a good deal of pressure, I do think it has helped up improve as trainers.

'I think Grant and I complement each other. He is the eyes on the ground and he looks after the horses and I ride them and see how they are feeling. The good thing is we both expect a high standard and don't except anything less. We have a gorgeous daughter named Tahni Maree, part-named after Maree Payne, and she's now seven years old and loves the horses.'

Williams is adamant that trainers need strong and loyal owners like Peters and Elio and Jacque Galante, who followed Grant over from the harness industry, for maintained success. Through Peters, she was introduced to the best horse with which she has been connected — champion mare Delicacy, winner of a Perth Cup, South Australian Derby, Australasian Oaks, Western Australian Derby and Western Australian Oaks.

In their first year as an official training partnership, Alana and Grant achieved quite remarkable figures and claimed the Perth trainers' premiership. They have managed a large number of winners while hovering around an exceptional runner-to-winner strike rate of around twenty-five percent.

'We have prominent owners but also some smaller ones and strike rate is important,' Williams says. 'We have a new bunch of young guys, first time horse owners, who the sport desperately needs for the ongoing success of the industry here in WA, who buy small shares in yearlings each year. And all the guys from the trots who followed Grant to the gallops, loyal owners. This is our crew, and we are proud of it. I would never have dreamt that it could have snowballed like this but it's come from hard work.'

As jockey Samson, her best win was in a Group 2 race for Bob Peters aboard class galloper Old Money. She may have eventually won that elusive Group 1 but the young woman who resumed riding just five weeks after fracturing her skull and C1 and C2 vertebrae in a Pinjarra race fall has no regrets.

'I always envisaged I would train one day and knew I didn't want to ride forever,' she says. 'It was hard on the body and my neck has given me trouble ever since the Pinjarra fall. I hope I did something to break the ice for other girls, I think I did and I think WA has become quite accepting of female jockeys. Girls never really got a chance to ride in the city before that but now things are a lot easier and much fairer all round.'

## Jockey

# LINDA MEECH

When Linda Meech isn't booting home a hundred winners a year, she's driving hours every day to country racetracks across Victoria that most of the metropolitan jockeys rarely visit. She's bought herself an apartment in Port Melbourne so she doesn't always have to make three-hour trips from her Stawell home when she picks up a few city rides.

For one of Victoria's busiest jockeys, the week comprises trackwork at courses from Stawell to Geelong, Seymour and Caulfield; attending to the very small team she's building since taking out a trainer–jockey license; a couple of nights in the city; five to six days riding right across the state; and a lot of time in the car getting there.

'There's no average week,' she says. 'I ride every Tuesday morning for Ciaron Maher but everything else is where I need to be. If Peter Morgan needs me at the farm or at Moonee Valley, I'm there. If he needs me to ride work at Sandown, I'm there. Sometimes I'm riding jumpouts at Mornington or Ararat. Unless you have a big stable you ride for, you have to be that busy.'

That's a lot of travelling around Victoria for someone who wasn't even born in the country. Meech hails from Pongaroa on the east coast of New Zealand's North Island and she rode her first winner at Rotorua in 1998. She came across later that year looking after several horses for trainer Kevin Myers and stayed with the Payne family in Ballarat. The amount of racing she saw was enough to convince her to stay. She switched her indentures from Wanganui trainer Janice Webster to Terry O'Sullivan at Stawell and then to Naracoorte conditioner Sue Jaensch. She rode all around the South-East of South Australia and the Western Districts of Victoria before moving to Sydney in the mid-2000s to ride for the all-conquering Gai Waterhouse stable while picking up rides for Paul Perry, Guy Walter and several other prominent New South Wales trainers. When she returned to Victoria, she built a very strong reputation as a class jockey with a great work ethic and forged a strong working relationship with leading trainer Peter Moody.

'When Pete stopped training, Ciaron Maher took over a lot of his horses and the owners have been happy to put me on,' she recalls. 'He's my most regular trainer and I also ride for Peter Morgan but I mostly ride for a lot of smaller trainers all over the state. I'm a freelance jockey who has some connections to a few stables, I guess you could say.'

That success provides some interesting figures for debate. More than 10,000 rides, 1400 winners, five one-hundred-winner seasons and a regular on Australia's top twenty jockeys list — sometimes the top ten. Meech has commanded respect through her riding deeds but perhaps one number gives away that she's a woman jockey. That number is eight. Somehow, almost inexplicably, she had ridden in just eight Group 1 races by the time she finished her nineteenth season.

Meech has managed to convert those limited opportunities into a Group 1 win — aboard Plucky Belle, the 2015 Coolmore Classic at Rosehill — which gives her a success rate of twelve percent at the highest level. Curiously, only the legendary Damien Oliver equals that among the leading Victorian riders. Even champion rider Craig Williams sits below ten percent winners to Group 1 rides. Other riders high on the metro premiership are struggling around the five percent mark. It's not as though she doesn't ride in the city as well as on the provincial and country circuits and it's not that trainers wouldn't be aware of her record, so what's keeping her out of the best races?

It can't have anything to do with ability. When Peter Moody had the immortal Black Caviar in the stable and was Victoria's leading trainer with the pick of virtually any rider, he secured Meech as one of his regular jockeys. He was a huge supporter, describing her at one time as 'the best horse in my stable' because of her great work ethic. Meech is philosophical about the Group 1 situation, preferring to concentrate on what she can control.

'It's definitely not because I'm out in the country because I spent seven years in town,' she says. 'There are also a lot of good male jockeys that can't get Group 1 rides. That's just how it is. It's probably public perception as to whether you're good enough and whether those owners want to put you on or not. If I had all the answers as to why I'm not getting the rides, I'd get the rides.

'It was a real highlight to win the Coolmore on Plucky Belle. I got the ride because I was riding regularly for Peter

Moody and [owner] Hamish Esplin has been a big supporter of mine. It didn't lead to more Group 1 rides from other sources, though, and I didn't really expect it would.'

While she can't do much about owners rating her worthy of Group 1 races, her work ethic and remarkable record ensures she picks up enough rides to be rated one of Australia's winningest jockeys. Meech is officially a jockey–trainer but she still considers herself very much the former while she rides out perhaps five more years. She prepares two horses on a four hectare property next to Stawell racecourse and she also has a couple of early two year olds she doesn't intend to rush. The stable is very small but she has no intention of expanding it too quickly while she remains one of Australia's busiest jockeys.

'I'm a little too busy race riding to deal with more than a couple of horses at the moment but I want to have the opportunity to train when I retire from race riding in four or five years,' she says. 'I can't race ride forever and I told myself I wouldn't ride past forty. I get bored easily so, while I don't have any lofty ambitions to run a big stable, I want to keep busy when I give away riding. I like working and I don't want to be uncompetitive so I will work hard to get results.

'I love Stawell and my property is perfectly located. It's not for everyone but it suits me and I like the idea that I can go fishing with my mates. Stawell is a good place to have a stable. If your horses aren't good enough for Melbourne, you can run them around the Wimmera or other parts of Victoria or even cross over to Mount Gambier and Naracoorte. I'll be keeping my Melbourne apartment but I can't see myself moving from Stawell.'

Linda Meech is remarkably humble. Perhaps too much so. She believes her success is built around hard work rather than the outstanding riding talent for which she is widely recognised. But whether she likes it or not, she has become arguably the most respected woman jockey in Australia and one the young girls coming through the ranks aspire to become. She's a fierce competitor but she also recognises her place in the industry and tries to support those girls coming through where she can.

'A lot of us jockeys have formed a bond over the years, male and female,' she says. 'But you get to know the girls really well. Some of them I've known since I was a kid and some of them are kids coming through and I suppose we're a bit of a family.'

Meech is respected by those who matter, even if it doesn't lead to a flood of Group 1 rides. She's always hopeful of picking up the occasional ride on a topliner for Maher or Morgan, who put her on brilliant young galloper Sircconi to win the 2017 Group 2 Sires' Produce at Flemington. In the meantime, the unassuming champion is content racking up a century of winners season after season.

Trainer / Jockey

## MICHELLE PAYNE

Never, in its 150-plus-year history, has the three-and-a-third minutes of the Melbourne Cup done so much to generate discussion and debate well beyond the industry.

Not only did Michelle Payne have to overcome biases that made her the only woman riding in the 2015 Melbourne Cup, she had to achieve her success on the despised outsider of the field. It's doubtful any rider in the world could have handled Prince of Penzance any better that day but the celebration around her success was that a woman finally won the race. Not the quality of the ride but the gender of the rider.

The media was all over Payne. She was on talk shows, morning television, international news services. Her 'everyone else can get stuffed' comments, aimed squarely at an establishment she argues has never given women riders a fair go, made her something of a feminist icon.

Media circus was the perfect description for what followed the Cup win. Some news reports referred to

Payne as the first 'lady rider' to win the Cup, unaware of the connotation it brings; others ran with the 'get stuffed' angle. Few remember a happy rider who said she was 'so pleased to win and hopefully it will mean more people give female jockeys a go'.

Payne's overall record was lost in the circus. This was no one-trick pony who happened to fluke a ride on a 100/1 shot. She had ridden almost 750 winners and the Melbourne Cup wasn't her first but her fifth Group 1 victory. She overcame life-threatening injuries early in her career when she was thrown head first into the Sandown turf in 2002, resulting in a fractured skull and bruising to the brain.

The youngest of trainer Patrick Payne's ten children, Michelle was a few months old when her mother Rosa Mary died in a car accident. It would be too simple to say she grew up tough: the reality is that everyone had to pull their weight from a young age. She was the baby sister looked after by siblings up to seventeen years older than her, seven of whom knew a thing or two about race riding. Among them, Brigid and Therese were groundbreaking jockeys in the eighties and Patrick Jr was a Group 1 winner turned trainer.

For all her success, the Melbourne Cup was something else again. She wasn't supposed to finish in the first ten on a dour handicapper who looked much better suited to a Group 3 staying race. But what should have been the dawn of a new era of success for Michelle Payne has not worked out that way at all. Winning the Melbourne Cup with a once-in-a-decade ride certainly hasn't earned her more rides, nor has it guaranteed her favour among the officials. Many argued Payne was too angry for someone who had reached the peak of Australian racing. Perhaps. Or perhaps speaking out of the perceived ills after achieving the ultimate success was the perfect forum? She cops plenty of criticism herself and, after criticising the state of the Flemington track and its curator on 2017 Australian Guineas Day, Racing Victoria slapped her with a $1500 fine.

Her comments were qualified though, saying she understood the racecourse manager had a tough job, but that having a small section of better going (or a fast lane) was unacceptable on a major race day. 'This shouldn't be happening so many times on our best track, which is a beautiful big, track,' she concluded her comments. One week later, Hall of Fame trainer David Hayes slammed the Australian Cup Day surface at the same Flemington track for the very same thing and received no penalty.

Within months of the Cup win, Payne suffered severe injuries in a race fall at Mildura, requiring pancreatic surgery and several weeks in hospital. She was again at odds with some of Prince of Penzance's owners when they opted to put another jockey on the gelding for his 2016 spring return in the Memsie Stakes. They steadfastly maintained they were concerned about her health and her condition and hoped she would take advice not to ride again; she insisted she was ready and that, as the only jockey to win aboard the now-retired stayer, she was the best option.

Having overcome serious injury and still fighting to secure rides, Payne has taken up training while still riding. The move has already met with obstacles. She was immediately stopped from riding her own horses in Sydney because of rules preventing trainer–riders.

Payne now trains up to fifteen horses at any time at her Nottingham Farm stables in Ballarat. She has teamed up with Australian Thoroughbred Bloodstock to launch Women in Racing, a syndication program controversially restricted to female investors. 'This association can deliver on some themes about women and racing that are very close to my heart (and) open the door for many, many more women to experience the thrill of part-ownership of a racehorse,' she said at the business media launch.

While the rides didn't immediately flow on from her greatest win, Payne's deeds were recognised beyond the racetrack — even an international feature film is planned. She was named Queen of Moomba in 2016 and shared in the festivities with brother and Melbourne Cup strapper Stevie, who was named King of Moomba the same year. She was awarded the coveted Don Award at the 2016 Sport Australia Hall of Fame Awards — an honour given to the athlete judged to have inspired Australians the most through sport in a twelve-month period.

The seasons to follow may not have been everything Payne imagined but that one faultless ride on racing's greatest stage at Flemington has earned her a place in the pantheons of Australian sport.

## THE AUTHOR

The plight of women in racing has intrigued Shane since he worked at the SAJC in his youth and heard colleagues dismiss visiting rider Therese Payne (Michelle's sister) as a 'sheila' who couldn't ride, even though she was an outstanding jockey who outrode many of the men.

Shane McNally has been a racing journalist and writer for thirty years. He started work writing for *Racetrack Magazine*, then *Turf Monthly*, *Thoroughbred Times* (in the US) and now for *Gallop* (in Europe). He also wrote the *Turf Heroes* documentary and has worked on radio and with Tabcorp as a tipster and contributor.

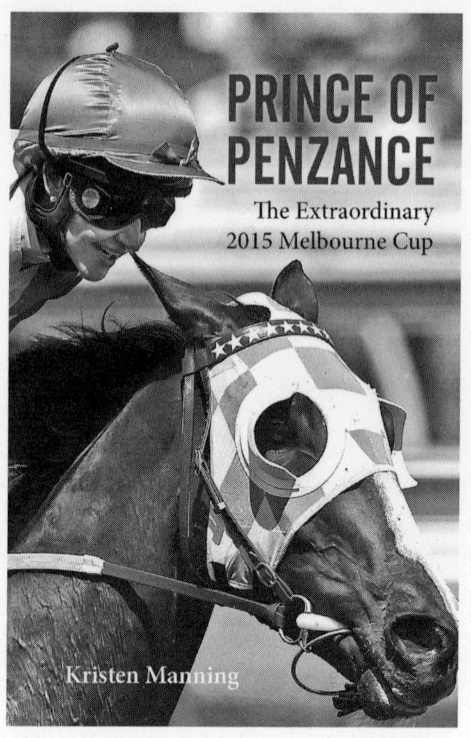


also by Melbourne Books

*Prince of Penzance:*
*The Extraordinary 2015 Melbourne Cup*

by Kristen Manning

available at bookstores and
*www.melbournebooks.com.au*